Microsoft Azure Storage Essentials

Harness the power of Microsoft Azure services to build efficient cloud solutions

Chukri Soueidi

BIRMINGHAM - MUMBAI

Microsoft Azure Storage Essentials

First published: August 2015

Production reference: 1250815

Published by Packt Publishing Ltd.
Livery Place
35 Livery Street
Birmingham B3 2PB, UK.

ISBN 978-1-78439-623-7

www.packtpub.com

Credits

Author
Chukri Soueidi

Reviewers
David Braverman
Sebastian Durandeu
Florian Klaffenbach
Laxmikant P. Patil

Commissioning Editor
Amit Ghodake

Acquisition Editor
Sonali Vernekar

Content Development Editor
Siddhesh Salvi

Technical Editor
Madhunikita Sunil Chindarkar

Copy Editor
Ting Baker

Project Coordinator
Nidhi Joshi

Proofreader
Safis Editing

Indexer
Hemangini Bari

Production Coordinator
Nitesh Thakur

Cover Work
Nitesh Thakur

About the Author

Chukri Soueidi is a software developer based in Beirut, Lebanon. With an experience that spans more than 8 years, he specializes in web development and Microsoft technologies. He currently works at the American University of Beirut as a software engineer and systems analyst, developing new software solutions for the university and its medical center.

He was awarded the Microsoft Most Valued Professional (MVP) award for 2 years 2014 and 2015 for his contributions to the technical communities of Visual C# and .NET. The MVP award is an annual award that recognizes exceptional technology community leaders worldwide, who actively share their high-quality and real-world expertise with other communities. With fewer than 5,000 awardees worldwide, Microsoft MVPs represent a highly selected group of experts.

He is heavily involved in local developer communities in Beirut, coaching on the latest technologies, and he is also a regular speaker at the major evangelism events held by Microsoft, Lebanon. He conducted several workshops for university students and professionals on topics of software development and gaming technologies. Chukri is also a technical trainer and has been working as an instructor at the regional learning centers.

Away from his laptop, Chukri is an avid marathon runner. He enjoys exploring new places and cooking with his beloved ones and friends. You can always reach him at chukrisoueidi@outlook.com.

Acknowledgments

I would like to take this opportunity to express my appreciation and gratitude to the Packt Publishing team for all their trust and support. The comments of the technical editor, reviewers, and proofreaders were so valuable in realizing this title. I would also like to thank my acquisition editor, Sonali S. Vernekar, and the content development editor, Siddhesh Salvi, for their professionalism, guidance, and patience.

Furthermore, I would also like to express my appreciation for my family and the people who supported me throughout this new experience: my friend Rami Sarieddine, who provided me with key remarks and also shared his authoring experience with me; also, my brother Rabih Soueidi, Michel Makhoul, Saber Shebly, and Mohamad Ghandour for their constant motivation and advice.

Above all, I would like to thank my dearest Lena Osseyran for her remarkable support, motivation, and all the good food while writing! Thank you all.

About the Reviewers

David Braverman is the chief technology officer of Holden LLC, a pioneer in sales performance development. Braverman is also an accomplished software developer and consultant with nearly 25 years of experience of working in the U.S. and Europe. Before joining Holden LLC, Braverman performed due diligence technology investigations of potential acquisition targets for West Monroe Partners, created and developed a healthcare scheduling application for medical interpreter businesses, wrote security analysis and reporting software, assisted a Portuguese mobile telecom provider with location-based service offerings, and led a large team that developed an inventory prediction application for an international food manufacturer. Braverman earned his MBA from Duke University, a JD from Loyola University Chicago with special recognition in intellectual property law, and a BA from Hofstra University. You can follow him on his blog, `http://www.thedailyparker.com/`.

Sebastian Durandeu is a senior software engineer with a primary focus on building applications and services for the cloud using Microsoft technologies. He works at Southworks, a high-end software development company that helps businesses leverage the latest technologies. Here, he has worked closely with several Microsoft divisions, helping the developer community adopt emerging technologies by using recommended practices. Sebastian currently lives in Buenos Aires, Argentina, where he is an active contributor to the developer community. He shares his knowledge via his Twitter (`@sebadurandeu`) and GitHub accounts (`sdurandeu`).

Florian Klaffenbach started his IT career in 2004 as a first- and second-level IT support technician and an IT salesman trainee for a B2B online shop. After this, he worked for a small company as an IT project manager, where he was involved in planning, implementing, and integrating industrial plants and laundries into IT enterprises. After spending some years there, he changed his path and worked with Dell Germany. There, he started from scratch as an enterprise technical support analyst and later worked on a project to start Dell technical communities and support over social media in Europe and outside the U.S. Currently, he is working as a solutions architect and consultant for Microsoft infrastructure and cloud, specializing in Microsoft Hyper-V, file services, System Center Virtual Machine Manager (SCVMM), and Microsoft Azure IaaS.

In addition to his employment, he is active as a Microsoft blogger and lecturer. He blogs on his own page, Flo's Datacenter Report, which can be viewed by visiting `http://datacenter-flo.de/`, and for the Brocade Germany Community. Along with a very good friend, he founded the Windows Server User Group Berlin in order to create a network of Microsoft IT professionals in Berlin. Florian currently maintains a very tight network that comprises many vendors, such as Cisco, Dell, and Microsoft, and communities. This helps him expand his experience and get the best out of a solution for his customers.

Florian has worked for several companies, such as Dell Germany, CGI Germany, and his first employer, TACK GmbH.

He has also worked on the book *Taking Control with System Center App Controller*.

I want to thank Packt Publishing for giving me the chance to review this book and my girlfriend for not killing me for spending lots of our free time on the review.

Laxmikant P. Patil is a senior technical architect on various Microsoft technologies. He has 13 years of experience building complex software systems, from devices that are run by Linux and Berkeley DB to cloud-based highly scalable systems and SharePoint-based portal and content systems. He has written many papers on cloud adoption, technology migrations, ERP integrations, knowledge management, and cost-effective designing areas. He's passionate about applying technology to business problems that will fit into customers' budgets. His dream project is to develop a platform for kids that will help them develop analytical and logical thinking abilities. In his spare time, he enjoys watching cartoons. He writes on his blog at `http://laxmikantpatil.com/`.

I would like to thank my family, especially my lovely wife, Vasudha, for her understanding and the sacrifices that she made when I was reviewing this book. Love you!

I would also like to thank the Packt Publishing team for believing in me and my work. It was a great experience working with you. Thank you, team!

www.PacktPub.com

Support files, eBooks, discount offers, and more

For support files and downloads related to your book, please visit www.PacktPub.com.

Did you know that Packt offers eBook versions of every book published, with PDF and ePub files available? You can upgrade to the eBook version at www.PacktPub.com and as a print book customer, you are entitled to a discount on the eBook copy. Get in touch with us at service@packtpub.com for more details.

At www.PacktPub.com, you can also read a collection of free technical articles, sign up for a range of free newsletters and receive exclusive discounts and offers on Packt books and eBooks.

https://www2.packtpub.com/books/subscription/packtlib

Do you need instant solutions to your IT questions? PacktLib is Packt's online digital book library. Here, you can search, access, and read Packt's entire library of books.

Why subscribe?

- Fully searchable across every book published by Packt
- Copy and paste, print, and bookmark content
- On demand and accessible via a web browser

Free access for Packt account holders

If you have an account with Packt at www.PacktPub.com, you can use this to access PacktLib today and view 9 entirely free books. Simply use your login credentials for immediate access.

Instant updates on new Packt books

Get notified! Find out when new books are published by following @PacktEnterprise on Twitter or the *Packt Enterprise* Facebook page.

Table of Contents

Preface

Microsoft Azure Storage provides a set of services that can be used by applications for data management and storage. By providing scalable, durable, and highly available services, this platform is remarkable for its design and rich features that can help you achieve all types of data management tasks, from the simplest to the most complex. For developers, it provides a rapid development environment that supports small to large-scale applications, and enables new scenarios on the cloud, server, mobile, and web. For IT professionals, it reduces the complexity of managing, protecting, and replicating data.

Microsoft Azure Storage Essentials is a jump-start book for developing applications using the different storage services. This book will teach you about the different characteristics of each service and how to utilize them in applications and perform basic programming operations on them.

The storage services are exposed through REST APIs which make them accessible to any HTTP enabled application; these APIs allow for platform specific client libraries to be implemented on top of them. This book will be focusing on Windows Azure Client Library for .NET using the C# language. We will deal with storing and retrieving unstructured data with blobs, and then move on to tables to insert and update entities in a structured NoSQL fashion. Then, we will explore Queues as a reliable messaging service; after that, we will show file storage that allows migrating legacy applications' data to the cloud; to end with, we will learn about transient fault handling and service monitoring.

This book is an introduction to Microsoft Azure Storage and also to developing applications that make use of these data management services.

What this book covers

Chapter 1, *An Introduction to Microsoft Azure Storage Services*, introduces the Azure Storage service and all the options associated with storage accounts.

Chapter 2, *Developing Against Storage*, provides an overview of how to manage the services and utilize them programmatically using many familiar development platforms.

Chapter 3, *Working with Blobs*, examines the blob storage service and the two different types of blobs. It then, moves on to how to create and manage blobs.

Chapter 4, *Working with Tables*, looks at the Table storage service as an alternative database solution that is designed for the purpose of storing massive amounts of flat data.

Chapter 5, *Designing Scalable and Performant Tables*, provides a deeper dive into tables, in terms of design patterns and tackling the need for speedy read and write operations.

Chapter 6, *Working with Queues*, introduces the Queue storage service as a messaging solution for communications between different apps.

Chapter 7, *Working with Azure File Service*, allows you to create mounted shares on virtual machines that can accessed using the SMB protocol or simple REST APIs.

Chapter 8, *Transient Fault Handling and Analytics*, deals with transient fault handling and retry policies, and also examines Storage Analytics that comes with storage services.

What you need for this book

Provided that you are using a modern and decent computer, you will need the following in order to run the code samples in this book:

- Windows 7 or above
- Microsoft Visual Studio 2012 or above
- SQL Server 2008 R2 Express Edition or above (for testing the storage emulator)
- Windows Azure Client Library for .NET
- Azure PowerShell
- Internet connectivity

Who this book is for

This book is intended for IT professionals and students, who are familiar with data management solutions and web development. If you are a developer, you should be familiar with C# and Visual Studio in order to utilize the code examples available in this book.

Conventions

In this book, you will find a number of text styles that distinguish between different kinds of information. Here are some examples of these styles and an explanation of their meaning.

Code words in text, database table names, folder names, filenames, file extensions, pathnames, dummy URLs, user input, and Twitter handles are shown as follows: "You can delete a created queue by calling the `Delete` method of the queue."

A block of code is set as follows:

```xml
<?xml version="1.0" encoding="utf-8"?>
  <StorageService xmlns="http://schemas.microsoft.com/windowsazure">
    <Url>storage-service-url</Url>
    <StorageServiceKeys>
      <Primary>primary-key</Primary>
      <Secondary>secondary-key</Secondary>
    </StorageServiceKeys>
  </StorageService>
```

Any command-line input or output is written as follows:

```
mkdir /azure-file-share
```

New terms and **important words** are shown in bold. Words that you see on the screen, for example, in menus or dialog boxes, appear in the text like this: " To create a console application open Visual Studio and navigate to **New Project | Templates | Visual C# | Console Application**."

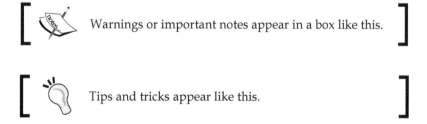

Warnings or important notes appear in a box like this.

Tips and tricks appear like this.

Reader feedback

Feedback from our readers is always welcome. Let us know what you think about this book—what you liked or disliked. Reader feedback is important for us as it helps us develop titles that you will really get the most out of.

To send us general feedback, simply e-mail feedback@packtpub.com, and mention the book's title in the subject of your message.

If there is a topic that you have expertise in and you are interested in either writing or contributing to a book, see our author guide at www.packtpub.com/authors.

Customer support

Now that you are the proud owner of a Packt book, we have a number of things to help you to get the most from your purchase.

Downloading the example code

You can download the example code files from your account at http://www.packtpub.com for all the Packt Publishing books you have purchased. If you purchased this book elsewhere, you can visit http://www.packtpub.com/support and register to have the files e-mailed directly to you.

Errata

Although we have taken every care to ensure the accuracy of our content, mistakes do happen. If you find a mistake in one of our books—maybe a mistake in the text or the code—we would be grateful if you could report this to us. By doing so, you can save other readers from frustration and help us improve subsequent versions of this book. If you find any errata, please report them by visiting http://www.packtpub.com/submit-errata, selecting your book, clicking on the **Errata Submission Form** link, and entering the details of your errata. Once your errata are verified, your submission will be accepted and the errata will be uploaded to our website or added to any list of existing errata under the Errata section of that title.

To view the previously submitted errata, go to https://www.packtpub.com/books/content/support and enter the name of the book in the search field. The required information will appear under the **Errata** section.

Piracy

Piracy of copyrighted material on the Internet is an ongoing problem across all media. At Packt, we take the protection of our copyright and licenses very seriously. If you come across any illegal copies of our works in any form on the Internet, please provide us with the location address or website name immediately so that we can pursue a remedy.

Please contact us at copyright@packtpub.com with a link to the suspected pirated material.

We appreciate your help in protecting our authors and our ability to bring you valuable content.

Questions

If you have a problem with any aspect of this book, you can contact us at questions@packtpub.com, and we will do our best to address the problem.

1
An Introduction to Microsoft Azure Storage Services

Microsoft Azure is an open and secure cloud platform that enables you to build, deploy, and manage applications. With its broad collection of services, it allows you to build with any programming language, tool, or framework, and integrate your cloud-hosted solutions with your existing IT environments.

Azure services fall into three main categories: **Infrastructure as a Service (IaaS)**, like virtual machines; **Software as a Service (SaaS)**, like Azure SQL; and **Platform as a Service (PaaS)** solutions, like Office 365. This is a collection of offerings that engage IT specialists, developers, and business owners.

The platform is globally present through a network of Microsoft-managed datacenters, distributed around 19 remote regions (as of writing), which facilitate redundancy and rapid recovery. It is a self-service platform where you can provision your resources and scale them elastically based on your own business needs.

It supports various programming languages such as .NET, PHP, Java, Node.js, Python, and Ruby. In addition, it supports a variety of data services like relational databases, NoSQL, and Big Data solutions. It also promotes hybrid solutions and allows you to extend your datacenters to the cloud using virtual networks.

Below is a brief classification for the services offered:

- Compute services such as virtual machines and cloud services
- Web and mobile services such as web apps and mobile apps
- Storage and data services such as blobs, tables, and SQL databases

- Hybrid integration services such as queues, BizTalk, and Service Bus

- Networking services such as virtual networks and traffic manager

- Analytics services such as machine learning

- Identity and access services such as active directory and multi-factor authentication

- Media and CDN services

Azure also offers management services, like the portal and marketplace, and developer enriching features such as Visual Studio Online and application insights.

For all services, you can check them out on the Azure documentation website at http://azure.microsoft.com/en-us/services/.

You can also download the service catalog poster from http://azure.microsoft.com/en-us/documentation/infographics/azure/.

An introduction to Azure Storage

Azure Storage is a highly-available and massively-scalable cloud storage platform that is designed to help you build internet scale applications. It is designed to store huge amounts of geo-redundant data with very fast performance. The platform exposes different abstractions of storage services to target different scenarios. This book will cover four service abstractions of storage, which are blobs, tables, queues, and file storage.

These services, like many other services from Azure, are exposed and accessed via REST APIs. Microsoft also provides a set of client libraries built on top of the REST APIs for different platforms like .NET, Android, and Node.js. These libraries facilitate interaction with the storage services, and add additional advanced capabilities like retry logic and asynchronous programming.

Azure Storage enables new scenarios for applications that require scalable and highly available data storage. These include applications such as social networks, video and image serving apps, gaming, medical records, and much more. Consumers will only pay for what they use based on traffic and capacity. Some of the Azure Storage key design features are described in the next sections.

High availability and durability

Azure Storage allows you to store petabytes of data, which will always be replicated to multiple locations. Microsoft guarantees 99.9 percent availability of the data when requested through SLAs, a topic we will discuss later. The periodic replication across geographically dispersed locations also ensures data recovery protection against disasters like earthquakes, fire, and so on.

Strong consistency

The service is designed to support a strong consistency model, which means that updates on the data are directly reflected to all replication locations where data is distributed. That is opposed to eventual consistency models that propagate changes eventually and not directly. The ability of Azure Storage to be highly available, strongly consistent and distributed is due to the advanced layering system and the design implemented in the storage platform.

Scalability

The major goal for the service is to enable the storing of massive amounts of data. For this, the service implements a global namespace, which makes access to the data consistent for consumers from any location in the world. You can scale to arbitrary amounts of data over time without worrying about where this data is stored and how it should be accessed.

 Other abstractions of the platform are Azure Disks and the Premium Storage service, which both deliver disk support for Azure Virtual Machines. In this book we will not use these services; our main focus will be the services that are needed by apps.

Storage services

As mentioned earlier, the service offers different kinds of abstractions that are intended to accommodate different data management and storage needs for applications. For unstructured data, there are Azure blobs; for structured non-relational data you have Azure tables; for reliable messaging between applications you have Azure queues; for standard file shares, there are Azure files.

The Blob storage

Blob storage provides a massively scalable object store in the cloud. This includes objects such as documents, large log files, backups for computers, databases, videos, and so on. Blobs are placed inside containers that can contain many of them, not exceeding 500 TB.

There are two types of blobs: *block* blobs, which are perfect for storing objects that might be streamed and used by applications like media files and documents. The other type is *page* blobs, which are optimized to support random writes like virtual hard disk drives.

The Table storage

Tables offer a highly available and scalable option for applications to store semi-structured datasets. They are ideal for apps that require a non-relational, flexible data schema like user, device, or any other type of metadata.

You can store key/attribute entities inside tables; tables are schema-less, meaning that you can store different types of datasets inside the same table, which allows to rapidly adapting to data changes in applications.

A NoSQL cloud store is currently being used by several types of applications that do not require relational databases. Data can be accessed using the standard REST interface and OData protocol for querying.

The Queue storage

Queue storage provides a reliable, low-latency and high-throughput messaging system. You can decouple components to create more flexible apps that are less sensitive to individual component failures by buffering operations into queues. Also, this allows you to handle traffic bursts by saving operations and not dropping them. It allows scheduling of asynchronous tasks such as large data operations or simply sending emails.

The File storage

File storage provides cloud-based file shares allowing legacy applications to make use of the cloud, which provides them with mounted shares. File storage can be used to store data that needs to be accessed by virtual machines, such as configuration and installation files. You can create shares and under them create directories and files, all of which are accessed via a REST API along with the standard file access protocol SMB, which we shall discuss later.

Storage accounts

The Azure storage account is the basic block of the storage service. It manages access to the storage resources and provides a unique namespace for them; it also defines how your data will be replicated and made redundant. In order to create a storage account you need a valid Azure. There are various ways to create storage accounts; the easiest way is from the Azure portal (Azure provides a management portal that we will discuss in later chapters). Following very simple steps, you will be asked to provide a URL, choose a desired location for your data, and a replication option. Another option to create a storage account is to do it programmatically by using one of the client libraries.

For a step-by-step tutorial on creating storage accounts from the portal, see https://azure.microsoft.com/en-us/ documentation/articles/storage-create-storage- account/#create-a-storage-account.

In the following sections we shall discuss the basic and essential features of storage accounts. The following figure illustrates Microsoft Azure Storage concepts:

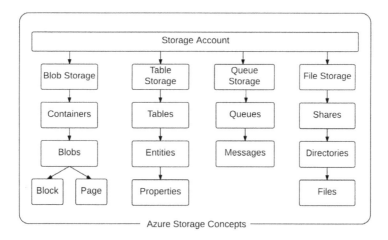

Azure Storage Concepts

The namespaces and endpoints

As mentioned earlier, each storage account has a unique global namespace, which allows clients to address the service resources. The storage account is a part of this namespace that represents a URI that can be called via simple HTTP and HTTPS requests.

Thus, all data is accessible via the following endpoints:

- **Blob service**: `http(s)://<account-name>.blob.core.windows.net`
- **Table service**: `http(s)://<account-name>.table.core.windows.net`
- **Queue service**: `http(s)://<account-name>.queue.core.windows.net`
- **File service**: `http(s)://<account-name>.file.core.windows.net`

The account name `<account-name>` is selected by the user creating it and should be unique among all other storage accounts. This name will be used by the platform to locate where the data is stored in order to route incoming requests.

Storage account security

By default, and for the security of your data, all requests to the storage service must be authenticated. To do this, the platform generates two access keys for each account that should be supplied for authentication. The owner of the subscription can regenerate any key at any time. By having two access keys, the user can use the second key to authenticate while generating a new one, so that no downtime or interruption will occur to the service.

It is recommended you do not share the access keys with other users; they should be kept safe. In order to allow other users to access your data, you can create **Shared Access Signatures (SAS)**. These signatures can be generated for a specific set of resources with a specific access permission for a definite amount of time.

> To gain full understanding of how shared access signatures work, have a look at the following link:
>
> `https://azure.microsoft.com/en-us/documentation/`
> `articles/storage-dotnet-shared-access-signature-`
> `part-1/`

You can also give public read access to blob storage in containers. When a container is set to public, anyone can read the data without authenticating the request. This is perfect for public media files such as images, documents, or videos on websites. (Users will still need valid storage access keys to write or delete data, however.)

> **Downloading the example code**
>
> You can download the example code fies from your account at `http://www.packtpub.com` for all the Packt Publishing books you have purchased. If you purchased this book elsewhere, you can visit `http://www.packtpub.com/support` and register to have the fies e-mailed directly to you.

Redundancy options

Azure Storage is available at several regions around the world, allowing data to be replicated within the same region or to different regions, depending on your selection. The following are the replication strategies to choose from when creating a storage account:

- **Locally redundant storage (LRS)** stores three synchronous copies of the data in a single facility in the same region.

- **Zone-redundant storage (ZRS)** is where data is stored and replicated across multiple facilities, either within one or two nearby regions.

ZRS is only available only for block blobs storage. Also, once you have created a storage account with ZRS, you cannot later change it. Further information can be found at `https://azure.microsoft.com/en-us/ documentation/articles/storage-redundancy/`.

- **Geo-redundant storage (GRS)** maintains six asynchronous copies of the data. Data is replicated the same way as for ZRS, but is then asynchronously replicated to a secondary far region that falls under a separate fault domain, without allowing direct access to it.

- **Read-access geo-redundant storage (RA-GRS)** provides all of the benefits of geo-redundant storage noted above, but it allows read access to data at the secondary region whenever the primary region becomes unavailable.

A fault domain is a collection of servers and network components that share a single point of failure. To improve service availability, Azure hosts data on multiple fault domains.

Metrics and logging

You can monitor your storage account by collecting metrics for the requests on your services. Metrics are collected to analyze usage and diagnose issues in order to improve performance of all consuming applications.

Transactional information such as ingress/egress, latency, and success percentages is saved for requests and responses on services. Capacity information is also stored to monitor usage. Data in these tables can be accessed using the table service APIs and .Net APIs. The data is read-only and cannot be manipulated or created by the user.

Summary

The purpose of this chapter is to introduce you to Azure Storage and make you familiar with its components and features. Through subsequent chapters, we will explore these topics more and dive into developing apps that consume Azure Storage service using the .NET framework. The next chapter will focus on the way this service exposes its functionality to consumers through Service APIs that allow developers to execute operations on the service platform from any client app.

2
Developing Against Storage

The Azure Storage platform exposes two REST APIs that allow you to operate on it, one for service management and the other for dealing with each service specifically. These APIs allow developers to interact with and consume the storage services programmatically from applications. The platform also offers multiple client-side libraries for application, under open source licenses that encapsulate the functions of the REST APIs in a higher level code. These libraries target most of the major programming platforms. This chapter will be centered on the different APIs available, and then on the major client libraries available.

The Service Management REST APIs

The first set of APIs we will discuss are the Service Management APIs, but before that we must mention the management portal. The Azure platform provides a centralized web portal that allows you to manage your subscriptions and services through its interface.

 As of 2014, a new portal was made available, which includes a number of improvements and enhancements such as integrated billing, advanced application lifecycle management and deployment automation features.

All operations that can be performed from the portal for managing the storage accounts in subscriptions can also be done programmatically through the Service Management API. Actually, the portal itself uses the same APIs under the hood to perform such requests.

This programmatic access to such functionality is much needed by cloud applications that are usually designed to support multi-tenancy. Many scenarios require the creation of separate storage accounts for different tenants (customers). The Service Management API is essential for providing automation for all provisioning processes, allowing applications to create and manage different storage accounts programmatically.

> At the time of writing this book, each Azure subscription has a maximum limit of 100 storage accounts, a number that can be increased by contacting the support team.

The Service Management API is an HTTP based REST (Representational State Transfer) web service. Usually, a RESTful web service exposes server data and functionality to clients as web resources that can be accessed by URIs through a set of defined operations. For our service, these operations should always be performed over SSL and should be authenticated using an X.509 v3 certificate.

Here is a list of operations provided by the Service Management API and can be performed on storage account:

- Check storage account name availability
- Create storage accounts
- Delete storage accounts
- Get storage account properties
- Get storage account keys
- List storage accounts
- Regenerate storage account keys
- Update storage accounts

We will now take one of these operations as an example and examine its HTTP request and response. The operation will be the **Get Storage Account Keys** which is used to return both secret keys of a specific storage account.

The request

The request uses the HTTP **GET** verb on the URI:

```
https://management.core.windows.net/<subscription-id>/services/
storageservices/<service-name>/keys
```

This specific operation does not require additional URI parameters but it requires the **x-ms-version** request header that specifies the version of the operation. For this operation the request header is x-ms-version: 2009-10-01. The request body is empty for this operation.

 Service Management API has multiple versions. With each operation you must specify the version you want to use by defining the x-ms-version request header.

You have to make sure that the request is always secure using HTTPS. The subscription ID is a unique guide specific for your subscription and can be retrieved form the portal.

The response

The response will include an HTTP status code, a set of response headers and the response body. A status code 200 will be returned if the operation was successful. The response header will contain the **x-ms-request-id** header, which is a unique ID that identifies the request ID made to the server.

The response body will contain the requested data. In the XML format, it might look like the following example:

```
<?xml version="1.0" encoding="utf-8"?>
  <StorageService xmlns="http://schemas.microsoft.com/windowsazure">
    <Url> https://management.core.windows.net/subscription-guid/
services/storageservices/storage-account-name </Url>
    <StorageServiceKeys>
      <Primary>primary-key</Primary>
      <Secondary>secondary-key</Secondary>
    </StorageServiceKeys>
  </StorageService>
```

 The server will send the response with a **Content-Type** header that specifies the format of the data, that is, MIME type. To tell the server what content you will accept, you can set the **Accept** header in the request headers.

The response header will contain three elements:

1. The request URI used to perform the operation.
2. Primary storage account access key denoted above as primary-key.
3. Secondary access key denoted above as secondary-key.

Microsoft Azure Management Libraries

As an extension for the Service Management API, the Azure SDK for .NET contains the Microsoft Azure Management Library, a .NET library that includes wrappers around the management API. The comprehensive library makes it easier for developers to automate, deploy, and test the cloud infrastructure and services as it wraps most of the Service Management API inside the **Microsoft.WindowsAzure. Management.Storage** library.

You can get the libraries by running the following command in the Package Manager console in Visual Studio:

```
PM> Install-Package Microsoft.WindowsAzure.Management.Libraries
```

This library provides a painless automation layer for your applications in contrast to directly accessing the REST API. It is built on top of very popular libraries such as **Json.NET** and **HttpClient**. It also comes with support for Portable Class Libraries that are used to target multiple .NET platforms, and supports **async** and **await** for asynchronous programming.

The Storage Services REST APIs

The second type of APIs to discuss are the Storage Services REST APIs which provide programmatic access to the four different services offered by Azure Storage: **blobs**, **queues**, **tables**, and **files**. These APIs can be accessed from the Internet, allowing them to be consumed from any kind of application that can send and receive HTTP requests and responses.

Every request to the Storage Service must be authenticated (except for reading public blobs); the services support a shared key authentication scheme with a required augmented signature string for enhanced security.

The service also supports the Shared Access Signature policy, which grants restricted access rights to each of its four services. These shared access signatures could be generated to clients who cannot be trusted on the storage account keys. The signature is created for particular resources, be it blob container, queue, table, or file for a specific period of time and defined permissions.

Azure Storage services definitely support **Cross-Origin Resource Sharing (CORS)**, which is an HTTP feature that enables applications running under different domains to communicate and access resources from other domains.

 For more details you can check the full documentation on MSDN. `https://msdn.microsoft.com/en-us/library/azure/ dd179355.aspx`.

The following sections explain the four service specific components of the API. But first, let us see the URI scheme for accessing the different services provided by the service.

Service	URI
Blob service	`https://<your-account-name>.blob.core.windows.net/`
Table service	`https://<your-account-name>.table.core.windows.net/`
Queue service	`https://<your-account-name>.queue.core.windows.net/`
File service	`https://<your-account-name>.file.core.windows.net/`

The `<your-account-name>` will hold the unique name of your storage account. The following figure illustrates Microsoft Azure Storage architecture. You can see how all the services are scoped to a storage account that provides access to the separate services:

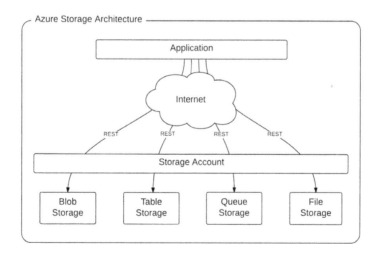

The Blob service REST API

This API exposes the Blob service as two resources: containers and blobs. It defines HTTP operations to deal with these resources, such as: list containers, create container, and get blob, put blob.

For example, a sample HTTP request for a get blob operation would perform an HTTP GET method on the following URI:

```
https://<your-account-name>.blob.core.windows.net/<your-
container>/<your-blob>
```

 The full list of operations that can be done using the Blob Service API can be found at: `http://msdn.microsoft.com/en-us/library/azure/dd135733.aspx`.

The Table service REST API

The Table REST API exposes the Table service components: the tables and their data entities. The API defines operations such as: query tables, create table, delete table, insert entity.

It also supports batch operations for entities operations, for insert, update merge, and delete.

The Table service REST API is compliant with OData specifications exposing the tables as resources via URLs such as:

```
http://< your-account >.table.core.windows.net/< table-name >
```

 The full list of operations that can be done using the File service API can be found at: `http://msdn.microsoft.com/en-us/library/azure/dd179423.aspx`.

The Queue service REST API

The Queue REST API exposes the Queue service as two resources: queues and messages. The API defines operations such as: list queues, create queue, delete queue, get messages, and delete messages.

A **get messages** operation would perform a GET on the following URI:

```
https:// <your-account-name >.queue.core.windows.net/your-queue/
messages
```

The full list of operations that can be done using the Queue service API can be found at `http://msdn.microsoft.com/en-us/library/azure/dd179363.aspx`.

The File service REST API

Shares, directories, and files stored in the File service are the resources accessible via the File service REST API. The API defines operations like: list shares, create share, create file, get file, set file properties, and so on.

The files stored in the Azure File service are accessible at the endpoint:

```
https://<your-account-name>.file.core.window.net
```

 The full list of operations that can be done using the File service API can be found at `http://msdn.microsoft.com/en-us/library/azure/dn167006.aspx`.

Azure Storage Client Libraries

Now we have seen how the Storage Service endpoints are exposed through the REST APIs that make them accessible by any platform using HTTP. These REST services provide a low level abstraction layer, which requires extensive filling of HTTP headers and repetitive work to be done by developers in order to execute operations. Microsoft provides several client libraries that give developers a higher layer of abstraction on these service. These object oriented libraries add extra functionality, like retrying policies that we will see later, and make developing with Azure Storage much easier. The rest of this chapter will list some of these libraries that target several platforms.

Microsoft Azure Storage Client Library for .NET

The .NET library allows you to access and execute operations on blobs, queues, tables and files from .Net applications. We will be using this library in the coming chapters to work with Storage Services.

Typically, in a .Net application, the library would be obtained using **NuGet**, which is the package manager for Microsoft development platform. The assembly that will be downloaded is **Microsoft.WindowsAzure.Storage.dll**.

For example, creating a blob container in C# would look like this:

```
// Retrieve storage account from connection string.
CloudStorageAccount storageAccount = CloudStorageAccount.Parse(
  CloudConfigurationManager.GetSetting(
  "myStorageConnectionString "));
// Create the blob client.
CloudBlobClient blobClient = storageAccount.CreateCloudBlobClient();
// Retrieve a reference to a container.
CloudBlobContainer container = blobClient.GetContainerReference("firs
tcontainer");
// Create the container if it doesn't already exist.
container.CreateIfNotExists();
```

Don't panic! In the following chapters we shall delve into these classes and use them extensively to operate on the four different Storage Services.

Microsoft Azure Storage Client Library for Node.js

This library makes consuming Storage Services easier from Node.js applications. It is a dedicated client library module that includes support to the full Storage Service REST APIs. It allows you to operate on the different Storage Services: table, blob, file and queue.

Creating a table using Node.js would look something like:

```
var azure = require('azure-storage');
var tableService = azure.createTableService();
tableService.createTableIfNotExists('yourstoragetable',
function(error, result, response){
  if(!error){
    // true if created; false if exists
  }
});
```

 To download and view full documentation of the SDK visit https://github.com/Azure/azure-storage-node.

The Microsoft Azure Storage SDK for Java

This Java Client Library provides easy access to Storage Services. Its basic object model is similar to Microsoft Azure Storage Client Library for .NET and designed in a way to be familiar to Java developers.

The packages are distributed per service. The main packages in the library are:

- `com.microsoft.azure.storage`: contains the package base classes and primitives such as `CloudStorageAccount`
- `com.microsoft.azure.storage.analytics`: contains classes to deal with the service analytics
- `com.microsoft.azure.storage.blob`: contains the Storage Service blob classes
- `com.microsoft.azure.storage.file`: contains the Storage Service file classes
- `com.microsoft.azure.storage.queue`: contains the Storage Service queue classes
- `com.microsoft.azure.storage.table`: contains the Storage Service table classes

 To download and view full documentation of the SDK visit `https://github.com/azure/azure-storage-java`.

The PHP Client Libraries for Azure

The PHP libraries provide an interface to access the Storage APIs, making it easier to access tables, queues, and blobs from PHP applications. It makes developing for Windows Azure from PHP an easy task for developers. These libraries are part of the **Windows Azure SDK for PHP** that wrap around the Storage Service API to add support to all of its operations.

 To download and view full documentation of the SDK visit: `https://github.com/Azure/azure-sdk-for-php`.

The Microsoft Azure SDK for Python

The SDK provides a set of packages to access Azure Storage Rest APIs from Python applications. It contains the **Python Client Libraries for Azure** that provides an interface to the Azure features.

The SDK is tested and supported on the CPython implementation since it's the standard and most common Python interpreter.

 To download and view full documentation of the SDK visit `https://github.com/Azure/azure-sdk-for-python`.

The Microsoft Azure SDK for Ruby

This library exposes the services provided by the Azure Storage REST API in a Ruby language specific library to ease the use of the API for Ruby developers. It contains the Windows Azure Data Management Library that provides wrappers for Storage Services.

 To download and view full documentation of the SDK visit `https://github.com/Azure/azure-sdk-for-ruby`.

Azure Storage Emulator

The Microsoft Azure SDK provides the Storage Emulator, a standalone package that provides a local environment for developers to emulate the Blob, Queue, and Table services on their machines. The storage emulator allows you to test the applications locally without any added cost. It uses a SQL server instance and the local file system on the computer to emulate the services.

The emulator has some limitations; it only allows one fixed pre-defined account and key. It also does not support large numbers of concurrent requests.

Addressing the emulator is slightly different than the Azure Storage, let us see in the following comparison how they differ. For referencing a blob in the Azure service you will use something like the following URL:

```
https://<your-account-name>.blob.core.windows.net/<your-
container>/<your-blob>
```

For storage emulator referencing, you will replace the namespace of the service with your local machine address and port as shown below:

```
http://<local-machine-address>:<port>/<your-account>/<your-container>/<your-blob>
```

PowerShell

Using Windows PowerShell, you can also work and execute operations on Storage Services. PowerShell gives you the ability to write and prepare scripts that can automate a bunch of operations required by you for multiple purposes such as creating storage accounts and preparing for deployment. These scripts will make sure that the same steps and operations are executed each time in the same order, reducing the effort needed to set up your environment.

> For a full list of cmdlets available you can check the following article: `https://msdn.microsoft.com/en-us/library/dn806401.aspx`

Summary

In this chapter, we have seen different ways to manage and access the Storage Services. The platform exposes REST APIs web services that can be consumed from any HTTP talking application. Microsoft also provides a lot of platform specific client libraries that wrap around these REST APIs and provide a higher level of abstraction that makes dealing with the Storage Services time effective and straightforward for developers. In the next chapter, we will demonstrate the first service, blobs, as part of the Azure Storage offering.

3
Working with Blobs

In this chapter, we will look into the Azure Blob storage service, which is designed for storing arbitrary unstructured binary data stored in file-like entities, or what is known as **Binary Large Objects (blobs)**. We will examine the structure of the two different types of blobs and where they are used, then we'll perform common create, read, update and delete operations on them.

Types of blobs

In general, files such as images, text files, media files, databases, backups, or virtual hard drives are typical examples of blobs that can be uploaded to the Storage Blob service. Blob storage offers two types of blobs: *block* blobs and *page* blobs. While creating a new blob, you have to specify its type, since each type has its own set of operations and features, we will talk about them separately in the following two sections.

Block blobs

A block blob is segmented into smaller chunks called blocks, each having a unique block ID. This allows you to upload blocks separately to the storage service, to then be committed into one single file, in what is called commit-based update semantics, which facilitates the transmission of larger files over the network. If any transmission failure occurs, it can be easily recovered by resuming the operation from the last successfully uploaded block.

Each block blob cannot consist of more than 50,000 blocks and cannot exceed a 200 GB maximum size, while a single block can have a maximum size of 4 MB. Block blobs are usually read from the first byte to the last, which makes them a preferable option for apps and websites that require the storage of different types of files. Client libraries that deal with blobs usually break files that are larger than 32 MB automatically into blocks before uploading them concurrently in multiple threads, removing any overhead for developers.

Page blobs

Page blobs, as their name suggests, are made up of smaller chunks called pages, each of 512 bytes. Page blobs are optimized for disks that need distributed access with random read and write operations. The size of the blob cannot exceed the maximum limit of 1 TB that is specified upon its creation, and while it is sparsely populated, you will be charged for the occupied pages in it. In contrast to block blobs, page blobs offer an immediate update allowing for faster range-based reads and writes.

 Page blobs are used by the platform in Azure Drives that provide a durable network attached drive for virtual machines.

The blob structure

The Storage Blob service consists of three main components:

- **Storage Account**: provides the namespace and manages access and authorization to all associated containers
- **Container**: provides logical groupings for blobs
- **Blobs**: are of two types (block and page blobs) and are always stored inside containers.

Containers

Blobs are always stored and organized into containers. A container can be either private or public, and specifies both the sharing and privacy level of the set of blobs it contains. Private containers require you to authenticate every request in order to execute any operation on its underlying blobs. Public containers allow anonymous reads to all blobs; but, of course, all write operations, such as create, update, or delete, should be authenticated.

Shared access policies can be applied on containers to provide more specific privileges and controlled access. A storage account can have an infinite number of containers, and containers can have an unlimited number of blobs, as long as the limit of 500 terabytes per storage account is not exceeded. Containers can also have their own metadata to store additional information in key/value properties.

Addressing blobs

Blobs and containers are addressed via URLs with the following pattern:

```
http://<account-name>.blob.core.windows.net/<container-name>/<blob-
name>
```

The `<account-name>` placeholder contains the storage account name, the `<container-name>` specifies the container name, and the `<blob-name>` specifies the requested blob name. Every single blob or container must have a unique name, and thus a unique URI per storage account.

Since containers are addressed via URLs, there are strict naming rules that apply. For container names, the name should be a valid DNS name, which means that a container name can only have alphanumeric characters in addition to dashes (-) that should be placed in between characters. Names should always be in a lower case and can range from 3 to 63 characters long.

For a blob, the blob name can contain any combination of characters with a range of 1 to 1,024 characters long. Blob names are case sensitive and preferably do not contain URL reserved characters. It is recommended to avoid blob names that end with a dot (.) or a slash (/). The forward slash can be used to create some virtual hierarchy, which we will see later in the chapter.

Using the Azure Storage Client Library

The Azure Storage Client Library for .NET has classes to manage and maintain blob storage objects using .NET languages. In the rest of this book, we will be working with C# language to demonstrate the storage services.

After creating a storage account, as discussed in earlier chapters, and getting one of the two account storage access keys we now have everything it takes to utilize the storage service using Visual Studio and C#.

For the simplicity of the demo's setup, we will be using a C# Console Application template. To create a console application, open Visual Studio and navigate to **New Project | Templates | Visual C# | Console Application**.

By default, the application does not have reference to the storage client library, so we need to add it using the package manager by typing `Install-Package WindowsAzure.Storage`. This will download and install the library along with all dependencies required.

> You can navigate through the library by expanding references in **Solution Explorer** in Visual Studio and right click on **Microsoft. WindowsAzure.Storage** and select **View** in **Object Browser**. This will show you all the library classes and methods.

After getting the storage library, we need to create the connection string by providing the storage account name and access key. The connection string would look like this:

```
<appSettings>
  <add key="StorageConnectionString"          value="DefaultEndp
ointsProtocol=https;AccountName=account name;AccountKey=access key/>
</appSettings>
```

```
In program.cs we need to reference the following libraries:
using System.Configuration; // reference to System.Configuration
should be added to the project
using Microsoft.WindowsAzure.Storage;
using Microsoft.WindowsAzure.Storage.Blob;
```

Creating a container

The following code gets the connection string from the `app.config` file. Depending on the type of application you are building, the connection string can be defined either in a `web.config` file in case you are developing an ASP.NET web application, or can be set using `CloudConfigurationManager` if you are using the Azure project template.

```
string connectionString = ConfigurationManager.AppSettings["Stor
ageConnectionString"];

CloudStorageAccount storageAccount = CloudStorageAccount.
Parse(connectionString);

CloudBlobClient blobClient = storageAccount.
CreateCloudBlobClient();
```

```
         CloudBlobContainer myFirstContainer = blobClient.GetContai
  nerReference("myfirstcontainer");

    myFirstContainer.CreateIfNotExists();
```

The preceding code then creates a `CloudStorageAccount` object, which wraps the storage account with its security credentials and endpoint addresses. This same object can be used while dealing with other Azure storage services like tables, files, and queues.

Then the `storageAccount` object is called to create a new `CloudBlobClient()`, which represents the Windows Azure Blob service that can be used to configure and execute requests. Then we created a `CloudBlobContainer` object, which every blob must reside in.

Uploading the first blob

We have already created a container reference in order to store our first blob in it:

```
  CloudBlockBlob blockBlob =
    myFirstContainer.GetBlockBlobReference("myblob");

          using (var fileStream =
            System.IO.File.OpenRead(@"path\localfile"))
          {
              blockBlob.UploadFromStream(fileStream);
          }
```

The preceding code gets a block blob reference and uses the `UploadFromStream` method on it to upload the stream of data collected by the `OpenRead` method. You can use any local file from your hard disk.

The `UploadFromStream` method will overwrite `myblob` if it already exists.

Getting acquainted with an explorer

A great way to make sure that your files are being uploaded to Azure is by getting a Windows Azure Storage Explorer. Most explorers show your data in a Windows Explorer fashion allowing you to create and edit blobs. It is a must have utility for its ease of usage, and access may help a lot in testing or even consuming your data.

A good list of available explorers can be found here:

`http://blogs.msdn.com/b/windowsazurestorage/`
`archive/2014/03/11/windows-azure-storage-`
`explorers-2014.aspx`

Downloading a blob

In order to download the blob into a file on your disk, we can use the `DownloadToStream` method on the blob reference.

```
using (var fileStream =
    System.IO.File.OpenWrite(@"Images\Chuck.jpg"))
{
    blockBlob.DownloadToStream(fileStream);
}
```

As we have seen in the *Addressing blobs* section in this chapter, blobs can be called by entering their URLs into any browser. So, in theory, pasting the following URL should download the file for us:

`https://<account-namename>.blob.core.windows.net/myfirstcontainer/`
`myblob`

The preceding URL will return to you a **Resource Not Found** error, which is due to the default private access level of the container. In the next section, we will dive deeper in this topic.

The container access level

Many cases where blobs should be shared by multiple anonymous users think of utilizing blobs as web content that needs to be referenced using HTML markup like images, CSS, or JavaScript files, which requires public access by browsers to the blob resource.

By default, containers and blobs are created with a private access level but they can be made to allow public read-only access.

In order to provide read-only access, we can do the following:

```
        myFirstContainer.SetPermissions(new
BlobContainerPermissions
    {
        PublicAccess =
            BlobContainerPublicAccessType.Blob
    });
```

The `BlobContainerPublicAccessType` is an enumeration that has three different values, which are:

Value	Public access
Off	Makes the container private and accepts only authenticated requests
Blob	Gives read-only public access to all blobs in the container
Container	Gives read-only public access to all blobs in the container, with the ability to iterate and list the container

The `Blob` enumeration value allows you to access blobs inside a container by addressing them by their direct URL. It does not allow public iteration of the container. Whereas, setting it to `Container` makes anyone see all the files in the container thus enabling the listing of blobs without authenticating.

Shared Access Signatures

The *container* access levels discussed earlier provide a very basic read-only access mechanism. Many times, you will need to give more permissions to third parties on your resources. Sharing the account key is not an option since it will jeopardize the security of the data in your storage account.

To handle this, giving adequate permissions can be achieved by generating a shared access signature. A SAS is a time-based generated string that defines a specific set of permissions and can be appended to the resource's URL. Shared access signatures are generated at the client side and not on the server. In order to create one, you must have one of the secret account keys.

A SAS usually contains: start time, expiry time, resource type, permissions, (read, write, delete, or list) and the signature which is generated by signing using the SHA256 algorithm the URL parameter with the storage account key.

Deleting a blob

A blob can be deleted programmatically by calling the `delete` method on its object reference:

```
blockBlob.Delete();
```

This may cause some issues if the blob has snapshots created for it. We will see how to handle that case later in this chapter.

Hierarchies

A storage account can be thought of as the root directory of a local hard drive on your machine. Containers are like folders that may contain other containers and many blobs, which are the files.

The $root container

As mentioned earlier, blobs must be stored inside containers, but for many reasons you might have to store them directly in the root container without referencing any container. An example of this might be the cross domain policy XML file that is required by several web clients in order to be granted permission to accept and handle data from other domains.

When a Silverlight application, for example, is requesting images from an Azure storage account, a `policy.xml` file should be present at the base URL of the storage account, where the data is available. This can be achieved by creating a root container that allows blobs to be addressed without adding any container name to the URL. The root container will act as a default container to the storage account, it must have the name `$root` and can be made available for public access.

The following URLs both work, provided the container is given public access:

* `https://<account-name>.blob.core.windows.net/policy.xml`
* `https://<accountname>.blob.core.windows.net/$root/policy.xml`

The folder structure

For saving and retrieving files, developers usually require a hierarchical structure along with blobs. By default, the blob storage service does not allow nesting containers making it a kind of flat file system. But applications do have a requirement sometimes where it is more convenient to have nested folders (containers) rather than a single layer of containers.

This can be achieved by simulating a directory structure and adding a forward slash (/) delimiter to blob names. For example, to create a nested hierarchy, in the following code we created a blob named `Folder1/insidefolderblob`. This will create the illusion of a folder that can be used programmatically to list all nested files inside it:

```
CloudBlockBlob blob = myFirstContainer.GetBlockBlobReference
    (@"Folder1/insidefolderblob");
blob.UploadText("This is a file inside a folder!");
CloudBlobDirectory dir =
    myFirstContainer.GetDirectoryReference("Folder1");
var files = dir.ListBlobs();
foreach (IListBlobItem item in files)
{
    Console.WriteLine(item.Uri);
}
```

As you notice from the preceding code, the Azure storage client library contains the `GetDirectoryReference` method inside the container object that automatically detects the nested files and directories.

Listing blobs

For listing blobs, the `ListBlobs` method navigates through a container and retrieves all blobs inside it. This method returns a list of `IListBlobItem` that can be casted into a page blob or block blob after checking its type.

To list all blobs inside a container:

```
foreach (ICloudBlob item in container.ListBlobs(null,true))
        {
            Console.WriteLine("Uri={0}", item.Uri);
        }
```

We have seen before how to create a folder-like structure inside a container. The `ListBlobs` blobs method accepts the `UseFlatBlobListing` parameter, which is set to `true` in the preceding code. When this flag is set to `true`, the method will return every single blob inside the container in a flat way, disregarding the folder structure you created using the slash (/) delimiter. When the flag is set to `false`, it will retrieve only immediate children blobs and virtual directories.

More options are available for enumerating blobs that allow you to filter results and specify the result count. These can be checked on Azure documentation.

Paged listing and continuation tokens

Normally containers would contain large amounts of blobs, which is one of the main reasons for using the service. Listing the contents of a huge container can result in a very big response, so it is preferable for the results to be retrieved in pages. Fortunately, the Client library provides the `ListBlobsSegmentedAsync` that returns the results in pages and provides a continuation token that can be passed to retrieve the next page.

Properties and metadata

There are two types of additional name/value properties that blobs and containers support, they are: metadata and properties. Custom metadata and properties can be set as HTTP headers sent with requests of creating or updating blobs or containers.

 By default, every container or blob has two read-only properties that are `Last-Modified` and `ETag`.

You can see how handy this could be in many scenarios. Consider the following previously discussed piece of code:

```
CloudBlockBlob blob = myFirstContainer.GetBlockBlobReference(
    @"Folder1/insidefolderblob");
```

The preceding code does not specify the extension of the requested `insidefolderblob`. If you view this file using the Azure Explorer, you will find that it has the content type of **application/octet-stream**, which only specifies that this is a binary file. This can be problematic for many client applications since, when the file is downloaded, the application will not be able to know what type is it and how to handle it.

To edit this property, you can do the following:

```
blob.FetchAttributes();
blob.Properties.ContentType = "text/plain";
blob.SetProperties();
```

 Another important property to fill is the `Cache-Control`, which allows the blob to specify its caching characteristics. This is pretty handy when dealing with static web content.

You may also want to add metadata to a blob in order to provide additional useful information to use later in your application. Suppose you want to add the name of the last user who updated a file. You can do this as follows:

```
blob.FetchAttributes();
blob.Metadata["LastModifiedBy"] = "Lena Osseyran";
blob.SetMetadata();
```

Conditional headers

In many cases, you need to perform low-cost conditional operations on blobs that are carried out only if a certain condition is satisfied. The storage service supports conditional headers that allow the service to validate these conditions on the server side thus saving a lot of time and avoiding unnecessary data transmission.

The supported conditional headers are:

Conditional header	Value
If-Modified-Since	DateTime Value
If-Unmodified-Since	DateTime Value
If-Match	ETag
If-None-Match	ETag

These headers can be used to perform conditional reads or conditional writes.

Blob snapshots

One of the many convenient features of the blob storage service is the ability to create snapshots of the blobs that can be used for tracking changes done on a blob over different periods of time. Snapshots provide an automatic and free versioning mechanism. They work by saving any changes done on the blob on a separate snapshot along with its timestamp. Using snapshots, you can rollback any changes done on a blob to a specific point in time or even to the original blob.

The following is an example of how to get a blob by specifying a snapshot value (provided that the container has a public access level):

```
http://<accountname>.blob.core.windows.net/<container>/<blob>?snapshot=timestamp
```

We will demonstrate how to create a snapshot by using the Azure Client Library. First, let us create a blob:

```
CloudBlockBlob blob =
  container.GetBlockBlobReference("hello.txt");
blob.UploadText("Hello world!");


In order to create a snapshot, we need to reference the
  original blob and call CreateSnapShot method:


CloudBlockBlob snapshot = blob.CreateSnapshot();
```

The snapshot object cannot be modified by itself; it only references a copy of the original blob at the time it was taken. We can then list all snapshots in a container as follows:

```
foreach (ICloudBlob item in mycontainer.ListBlobs(null,true,BlobListin
gDetails.Snapshots))
            {
            Console.WriteLine("Name={0}, Snapshot time={1}", item.
Name, item.SnapshotTime );
            }
```

You can also clone a specific snapshot into a new blob by using the `StartCopyFromBlob` method. First, you create an empty new blob and then copy the content of the referenced snapshot into it.

```
CloudBlockBlob newblob = container.GetBlockBlobReference("hello-copy.
txt");
newblob.StartCopyFromBlob(snapshot);
```

 When deleting a blob that already has snapshots, you should set the `DeleteSnapshotsOption` to include snapshots or else the delete operation will throw a `Microsoft.WindowsAzure.Storage.StorageException`

To delete a blob with snapshots:

```
blob.Delete(DeleteSnapshotsOption.IncludeSnapshots);
```

Summary

In this chapter, we looked into the blob storage service, which offers a really helpful service for storing and managing your unstructured data. We have covered all the essentials in this chapter. It is recommended that you have a look at the official documentation if you are planning to use blobs in your next project. The next chapter will be dealing with tables, which provide a scalable data store for keeping structured data.

4
Working with Tables

This chapter covers another service offered by Microsoft Azure. In the previous chapter, we have seen blobs, which provide a great option for storing unstructured data. The topic of this chapter will be Table storage. Tables provide scalable, structured data stores that allow you to store huge amounts of data. With the growing needs of modern high-performance applications, choosing the right data store is a major factor in the success of any application. We will start this chapter by discussing some of the data storage options and then dive deeper into the Table service.

The arrival of NoSQL

All software applications deal with data and eventually might need to store it somewhere and retrieve it later. When talking about databases, most developers first think of **Relational Database Management Systems** (**RDBMSs**) because that's how the market has been evolving for the past 40 years.

Traditionally, applications store data using relational database models organized into schemas, which are collections of related tables and views that describe the exact structure of the data. Much time and effort has been put into building and maintaining solutions using reliable and consistent relational database systems, such as Oracle, Microsoft SQL Server, MySQL, and many others.

Nowadays, applications should be able to serve millions of users from all over the world, dealing with information of extreme sizes. With the exponential growth of data, databases now need to allow for simple data operations with very good scalability, even if they are distributed over multiple servers.

Relational databases, in general, have little ability to scale; specifically horizontal scaling, meaning that they don't have the ability to distribute data and operations over a set of separate servers (with no shared memory). The main focus on their initial design was to provide ACID transactions. **ACID** is a set of principles that govern database transactions. It is a very broad topic but, in summary, **A** stands for **Atomic** ("all or nothing", which means that when performing an operation it either succeeds or fails as a whole), **C** is for **Consistent** (meaning that after operations the data should always be valid according to the constraints and schema), **I** is for **Isolated** (which means that operations are not visible to each other), and **D** is for **Durable** (which means that after an operation, data should be persisted with the ability to restore after failures).

According to Eric Brewer's CAP theorem, a system can only have two out of the three following properties: consistency, availability, and partition tolerance. Only by giving up one or more ACID principles, can systems achieve higher scalability and performance.

As data sizes increased massively, organizations had no choice but to give up on relational databases and start building alternative data stores to meet scalability and performance requirements. This led to what we call NoSQL databases; an ever-expanding list of data stores that give up some features to obtain others. They differ in their data models, storage and consistency mechanisms, and availability.

We will discuss the major types of these stores later, but, first, what is NoSQL?

NoSQL

Not Only SQL (NoSQL) databases are non-relational and mostly do not require SQL language to interact and manipulate data. These databases are intended to be simply designed and provide the highest scalability and availability, along with the ability to perform very fast read/write operations on huge amounts of data. NoSQL databases generally provide the following features:

- The ability to scale operations over many servers
- The ability to distribute data over multiple servers
- A simple interface or API to manipulate data (rather than strict SQL syntax)
- The ability to add new records dynamically

NoSQL databases fall under several categories, which we will discuss in the following section:

- **Key/value** databases are the simplest form of NoSQL databases, in which data is stored as tuples. Each record consists of this pair: a unique key used to identify the record and a scalar value of the data. The values are referenced by an attribute name. These databases are suitable for storing large amounts of data in scenarios where you want to query data based on the key and not on other columns in the table. In fact, Azure Table, our main topic for this chapter, is a key/value database.

- **Document** database is a key/value type database in which data is stored as documents. Values in documents can be scalar data, lists, or other nested child documents. The attributes are not defined in a specific schema and attribute names are dynamically defined at runtime. Data is usually stored as XML or JSON. Document databases define secondary indexes and are suitable for querying fields other than the key. MongoDB and CouchDB are the most popular document databases. For Azure applications, Microsoft recently launched DocumentDB: a NoSQL document database implementation that includes rich indexing features and full .NET support.

- **Column-family** databases store data as tuples with the ability to add families for a set of related columns in a single record. These families can be then partitioned on separate servers while keeping all these partitions related to one key. Cassandra and HBase are the most popular column-family databases.

- **Graph** databases store data as a collection of entities and relations. As the name suggests, these databases are intended to query nodes based on relationships between them. Think of Facebook, for example. Neo4j and OrientDB are the most popular.

 For more information on this topic, I recommend reading the *Scalable SQL and NoSQL Data Stores* paper written by Rick Cattell.

The Table storage basics

Azure Table storage is a key/value NoSQL database that allows you to store non-relational, structured, and semi-structured data that does not have to conform to a specific schema. It is ideal for storing huge amounts of data that is ready for simple and quick read/write operations, and is interfaced by the Table REST API using the OData protocol.

A table can contain one or many entities (rows), each up to 1 MB in size. The whole table cannot exceed a 100 TB limit. Each table entity can hold up to 252 columns. Rows in the same table can have different schemas, as opposed to relational database rows that should all comply under one strict schema.

Table storage is structured in a hierarchical relationship between storage accounts, tables, and entities. A storage account can have a zero or more non-related tables, each containing one or more entities.

The components of the service are:

- **Storage account**: Governs access to the underlying service
- **Table**: A collection of entities
- **Entity**: A set of properties, a row in the table
- **Properties**: Key/value pairs that can hold scalar data such as string, byte array, guid, dateTime, integer, double, boolean
- **Table address**: `http://<account-name>.table.core.windows.net/<table-name >`

The address differs when using the Storage Emulator, which emulates the Table storage service locally without incurring any cost. The default address will be the local machine loopback address followed by a predefined default storage account name. It would look as follows:

`http://127.0.0.1:10002/devstorageaccount1/<table-name>`

For more on the Storage Emulator, you can check out the *Use the Azure Storage Emulator for Development and Testing* article on the Azure documentation.

Entities

Entities, in tables, are associated with two key properties: the `PartitionKey` and the `RowKey`, which together form the entity's **primary key**.

The `PartitionKey` must be a string with a maximum allowed size of 1,024 characters. As its name suggests, it divides the table logically into partitions. Entities with the same partition key will be always stored in the same physical node, promoting performance and scalability.

When a table scales up, the Azure platform may automatically move different partitions of a table into separate physical storage nodes for load balancing purposes. Entities with the same partition key stay on the same node no matter how much their table scales; hence, the key selection is essential in determining the general performance of the table.

The second column is the `RowKey`, which is also of the string type, with a maximum allowed size of 1,024 characters. It has to be unique inside a partition, since the partition key and row key combine to uniquely identify an entity within the table.

In addition to that, each entity has a read-only mandatory `Timestamp` property, which is essential for managing concurrent updates on records.

Naming rules

When naming tables and properties, there are some naming rules to follow:

- **Tables**: A table name should be unique per storage account, ranging from 3 to 63 characters long. It can only contain alphanumeric characters and cannot begin with a number. Table names are case-insensitive, but will reflect the case that was used upon creation. (`Mytable` and `MyTable` are logically the same name, but if you create a table called `Mytable` then `Mytable` — not `MyTable` — will be displayed when you retrieve table names from the account.)

- **Properties**: A property name is case-sensitive with a size of up to 255 characters. It should follow C# identifier naming rules. When passed within a URL, certain characters must be percent-encoded, which is automatically done when using the .NET Library.

 Some characters are disallowed in the values of the row and partition keys, including the back slash (\), forward slash (/), the number sign (#) and the question mark (?).

Using the Azure Storage Client Library

The Azure Storage Client Library for .NET has classes to manage and maintain Table storage objects. After creating a storage account, as discussed in earlier chapters, and getting the appropriate account storage access keys, we now have everything it takes to use the storage service.

For the simplicity of this demo's setup, we will be using a C# Console Application template. To create a Console Application open Visual Studio and navigate to **New Project | Templates | Visual C# | Console Application**.

By default, the application does not have a reference to the storage client library, so we need to add it using the **Package Manager** by typing `Install-Package WindowsAzure.Storage`. This will download and install the library along with all dependencies required.

 You can navigate through the library by expanding **References** in Solution Explorer in Visual Studio, right-clicking on **Microsoft.WindowsAzure.Storage**, and selecting **View** in **Object Browser**. This will show you all library classes and methods.

After getting the storage library, we need to create the connection string by providing the storage account name and access key. The connection string would look like this:

```
<appSettings>
  <add key="StorageConnectionString"
    value="DefaultEndpointsProtocol=https;AccountName=account
name;AccountKey=access key/>
  </appSettings>
```

In `program.cs` we need to reference the following libraries:

```
using System.Configuration;  // reference to System.Configuration
should be added to the project using Microsoft.WindowsAzure.Storage;
using Microsoft.WindowsAzure.Storage.Table;
```

Starting with a table

Using the connection string defined in the `App.config` file, we will proceed to create a `CloudStorageAccount` object which represents the storage account where the tables will be created. After that we need to use the `CloudTableClient` class, which is defined under the `Microsoft.WindowsAzure.Storage.Table` namespace, to create an object which represents a frontage for dealing with Table storage specifically and directly.

After creating the table object we will call its `CreateIfNotExists()` method that will actually call the Table REST API to create a table. The method is idempotent: if the table already exists, the method will do nothing no matter how many times you call it.

The following is the code to do create a table:

```
string connectionString = ConfigurationManager.AppSettings["StorageCon
nectionString"];
    CloudStorageAccount storageAccount = CloudStorageAccount.
Parse(connectionString);

    CloudTableClient tableClient = storageAccount.
CreateCloudTableClient();

    CloudTable table = tableClient.GetTableReference("Weather");
    table.CreateIfNotExists();
```

A table can be deleted using the following code:
```
table.DeleteIfExists();
```

We created a `Weather` table for the purpose of demonstrating a broader overview of Table storage features. Our sample is a table for saving the weather history of all the cities around the world. For each city, the table holds a weather entry per day and time. Assuming there are more than 200,000 cities and each city has 24 entries per day, the table will contain millions of records in no time.

Adding entities to a table

After creating the table, `Weather`, we need to populate it with entities.
In the .NET library, entities are mapped to C# objects. The library defines
the `ITableEntity` interface which should be implemented by all classes
representing entities.

The `ITableEntity` interface defines the following properties:

- `PartitionKey`: It is a string for the partition key of the an entity

- `RowKey`: It is a string for the row key

- `Timestamp`: It is a `DateTime` offset for the last update on the entity

- `ETag`: It is an entity tag for managing concurrency

The library also contains two classes that implement `ITableEntity`.

The `TableEntity` is a base class that can be inherited by custom classes. The
`DynamicTableEntity` is a class that holds an `IDictionary<String,EntityProperty>` property named `Properties` that is used to store properties inside it.

Now, let's define our custom entity by inheriting from the `TableEntity` base class:

```csharp
public class WeatherEntity : TableEntity
{
  public WeatherEntity(string cityId, string daytime)
  {
    this.PartitionKey = cityId;
    this.RowKey = daytime;
  }

  public WeatherEntity() { }

  public string CityName { get; set; }
  public string CountryCode { get; set; }
  public string Description { get; set; }
  public string Temperature { get; set; }
  public string Humidity { get; set; }
  public string Wind { get; set; }

}
```

In the preceding code, we have defined the Weather entity class with a constructor that takes the arguments of cityId and a string representing the day and time, which we chose to declare as PartitionKey and RowKey, respectively; since the entity should inherit from a TableEntity class, we assign the keys to the base class properties using this.

 The partition and row key selection was based on the table's querying needs; we will discuss this topic in more detail in the next chapter. The PartitionKey is selected to be the cityId, and the RowKey is a string representation of the date and time in the format "yyyyMMddHHmm".

Now, after defining the entity as an object, we will proceed to add the entity to the WeatherHistory table. First we have to create an instance of this object and populate its properties, then hand it to a TableOperation object to insert it in to our table. The following is the code for this:

```
WeatherEntity weather = new WeatherEntity("5809844", "201503151200")
{
    CityName = "Seattle",
    CountryCode = "US",

    Description = "Clear",
    Temperature = "25.5",
    Humidity = "44",
    Wind = "11 km/h",


};

TableOperation insertOperation = TableOperation.Insert (weather);

table.Execute (insertOperation);
```

The TableOperation class represents a single table operation. In addition to the insert operation, this class defines the static merge, replace, and delete, and other methods that we will see later on. After creating the operation, we pass it to the Execute method of the CloudTable table entity, which represents the Weather table.

> The Timestamp property of the entity is required, but we did
> not set it in our code. This is because this property will be filled
> by the server automatically; even if we set it the server will
> rewrite its own timestamp.

Entity Group Transactions

In case we have several entities to insert into the table, we have the option to
perform a batch operation that can insert many records in one group transaction.
We can use the TableBatchOperation and add the entities to it, then perform the
CloudTable.ExecuteBatch.

The following is some sample code to add two weathers at the same time:

```
TableBatchOperation batchOperation = new TableBatchOperation();

WeatherEntity weather1 = new WeatherEntity("5809844",
"201503151300")
  {
    CityName = "Seattle",
    CountryCode = "US",

    Description = "Light Rain",
    Temperature = "23",
    Humidity = "82",
    Wind = "16 km/h",


  };

WeatherEntity weather2 = new WeatherEntity("5809844",
"201503151400")
  {
    CityName = "Seattle",
    CountryCode = "US",

    Description = "Heavy Rain",
    Temperature = "20",
    Humidity = "95",
    Wind = "16 km/h",
```

```
};

batchOperation.Insert(weather1);
batchOperation.Insert(weather2);
table.ExecuteBatch(batchOperation);
```

The following is a sample of how the table will look when it contains records for several days and cities; we omitted the timestamp for the clarity of the sample:

PartitionKey	RowKey	City	Country	Description	Temp.	Humidity	Wind
...	...	...	...	...	...	...	...
276781	201503151300	Beirut	LB	Clear	25	65	5 km/h
276781	201503151400	Beirut	LB	Clear	26	65	5 km/h
5128638	201503151300	New York	US	Sunny	25	46	11 km/h
5128638	201503151400	New York	US	Few clouds	25	46	11 km/h
5809844	201503151300	Seattle	US	Light rain	23	82	16 km/h
5809844	201503151400	Seattle	US	Heavy rain	24	95	16 km/h
6173331	201503151300	Vancouver	CA	Scattered clouds	6	84	12 km/h
6173331	201503151400	Vancouver	CA	Haze rain	5	84	12 km/h
7284824	201503151300	Budapest	HU	Light rain	4	80	14 km/h
7284824	201503151400	Budapest	HU	Light rain	4	81	14 km/h
...	...	...	...	...	...	...	...

Batch operations are quite an interesting feature of Tables, as they provide quasi-ACID transactions in the Table storage. Batch operations require all the entities included to have the same partition key or else an exception will be thrown.

 Batch operations can perform inserts, updates, and deletes in the same operation, and can include up to 100 entities with a payload size of 4 MB only.

Updating entities

In order to update an entity, we need to retrieve it first, then modify its properties to save it back again. `TableOperation` supports two types of updates: `Replace` and `Merge`. If the entity was modified between the retrieval and saving, an error will be generated and the execution of the operation will fail.

The `Replace` method will replace the values of the properties of an existing item with the object we provide. Have a look at the following code that changes an existing record for Seattle city for a specific day and hour:

```
    TableOperation retrieveOperation = TableOperation.
  Retrieve<WeatherEntity> ("5809844", "201503151300");

    TableResult result = table.Execute(retrieveOperation);

    WeatherEntity updateEntity = (WeatherEntity)result.Result;

    if(updateEntity != null)
    {
       updateEntity.Temperature = 26;
       TableOperation updateOperation = TableOperation.
  Merge(updateEntity);
       table.Execute(updateOperation);
    }
```

Notice in the preceding code that the `TableOperation.Retrieve` method takes the partition key with the row key as arguments, and retrieves the entity into a `TableResult` object that contains the `Result` property that can be casted into a `WeatherEntity` object.

But that's not all, changing an existing property in an entity is not the only type of update that may be required. As we have discussed previously, tables are schema-less, allowing entities in the same table to have different properties, which also means that you can add or remove columns even after the creation of a record.

Suppose you want to add more properties to a weather record, you can achieve this by modifying the class `WeatherEntity` and adding the new properties to it.

But what if you don't want to change the class since it's a rare collection of data that you are adding? This is where `Merge` steps in: it allows you to merge changes with an existing entity without overwriting old data.

```
    TableOperation retrieveOperation = TableOperation.
  Retrieve<WeatherEntity> ("5809844", "201503151300"); //all records for
  Seattle at March 15, 2015

    TableResult result = table.Execute(retrieveOperation);
```

```
WeatherEntity originalEntity =(WeatherEntity)result.Result;

if (originalEntity != null)
{
  DynamicTableEntity dynamicEntity = new DynamicTableEntity()
  {
    PartitionKey = originalEntity .PartitionKey,
    RowKey = originalEntity .RowKey,
    ETag = originalEntity .ETag,
    Properties = new Dictionary<string, EntityProperty>
    {
      {"Visibility", new EntityProperty("16093")},
      {"Pressure", new EntityProperty("1015")}
    }
  };
  TableResult results = table.Execute(TableOperation.
Merge(dynamicEntity ));
}
```

The preceding code gets an existing weather entity and assigns it to the
originalEntity, object. Then it creates a new object, DynamicTableEntity
and copies the PartitionKey, RowKey, and ETag to the new object and adds two
properties, Language and Country, as defined previously. TableOperation.Merge
was executed over the newly created object.

What this code does is that it adds two properties to the weather record without
changing other existing properties. If we had used Replace instead, the original
WeatherEntity properties CityName, CountryCode, Description, Temperature,
Humidity, and Wind would have lost their values.

Copying the three properties PartitionKey, RowKey,
and ETag (for optimistic concurrency) to the newly created
DynamicTableEntity is mandatory and without it the
operation would have failed.

Our `Weather` table now looks like this:

PartitionKey	RowKey	City	Country	Description	Temp.	Humidity	Wind	Visibility	Pressure
....	...	...	...	...	...	...	...		
5128638	201503151400	New York	US	Few clouds	25	46	11 km/h		
5809844	201503151300	Seattle	US	Light rain	23	82	16 km/h	16093	1015
5809844	201503151400	Seattle	US	Heavy rain	24	95	16 km/h		
6173331	201503151300	Vancouver	CA	Scattered clouds	6	84	12 km/h		
...	...	...	...	...	...	...	...		

As mentioned earlier, operations will fail if the entity has changed between the retrieval and the update. Sometimes you are not sure if the object already exists on the server or not. You might need to overwrite or insert your values regardless; to do that you can use the `InsertOrReplace` operation. This will overwrite your values even if they were changed, and if the record doesn't exist it will be inserted.

> Deleting an entity can be achieved after retrieving it, as follows:
> ```
> TableOperation deleteOperation = TableOperation.
> Delete(originalEntity);
> ```

Querying the table

Now, after we have persisted data in the table, we will start looking at ways of querying data from the server. Querying data should be our main concern when designing our tables in order to achieve maximum performance and avoid performance pitfalls.

Remember that tables are designed to store large amounts of records with extremely fast read/write operations; there are no relations between tables and thus no complex joins or queries.

Table service REST API supports querying the tables by performing `GET` operations; the service is actually a partial implementation of the OData protocol. All requests should be authenticated using `HTTPS`; responses from the service can be retrieved in **Atom Pub**, **XML**, or **JSON** format depending on the HTTP request header.

An authenticated request to get all tables under a storage account might have a URI as follows:

```
https://<account-name>.table.core.windows.net/Tables
```

To get all entities in a table, the URI would look like:

```
https://<account-name>.table.core.windows.net/Weather ()
```

But retrieving all the data in a table isn't something common for applications; usually applications query for subsets of data instead of retrieving the full dataset which costs a lot in terms of performance and charges. Due to the OData implementation, the service supports the following querying options that can help you limit the number of records returned by your queries:

Option	Description
`$filter`	Applies up to 15 comparisons with the `$filter` string and returns matching results. Supported
`$top`	Returns the top *n* results.
`$select`	Returns only the selected properties (server side projection).

The .NET client library provides an object-oriented abstraction over the REST service, hiding much of the complexity. Thankfully, the .NET library supports using some of the capabilities of the popular **Language-Integrated Query** (**LINQ**), which allows you to write and shape the results of a query in a more natural syntax. We will now demonstrate some examples that reflect different querying needs by applications.

Our first example will be querying based on the partition key. For example, the code below shows how to perform a `$filter` on a table by its partition key, in our case the `cityId`, and it will retrieve all entities in the city:

```
    IQueryable query = (from weatherRow in table.
  CreateQuery<WeatherEntity>()
    where  weatherRow.PartitionKey == "5809844"
    select  weatherRow);
  //all records for Seattle
```

The preceding code shows a LINQ query that is created using the `CloudTable.CreateQuery <TableEntity>()`. The `where` defines the filters and the `select` specifies the returned value (in this case the whole entity). At this point, the resulting `IQueryable` did not invoke a service and no calls are yet made to the server. In order to execute the query we need to enumerate the object by using `query.ToList()` or by enumerating the query object; for example, by a `foreach`. The results will be returned from the server sorted by the primary key (which is the `PartitionKey`, then the `RowKey`).

This query was retrieved as an `IQueryable`, which can be converted into a `TableQuery` object that can handle much more complex functionality. We will talk about it later in this section.

Our second example will be querying on both keys. In terms of performance, querying a table using both keys will achieve the best performance since it will be using its clustered index (an index that reorders the way records are stored physically) and will get your data in the quickest way.

In a case where you are using both keys, you can directly use `TableOperation.Retrieve()`:

```
TableOperation retrieveOperation = TableOperation.
Retrieve<WeatherEntity> ("5809844", "201503151300"); //all records for
Seattle at March 15, 2015

TableResult result = table.Execute(retrieveOperation);
```

Using the `where` in a LINQ query (like in the first example) will use the `$filter` query option on the table and generate the following HTTP request:

`https://<account-name>.table.core.windows.net/Weather()? $filter=PartitionKey%20eq%20'5809844'%20and%20RowKey%20eq%20'201503151300'`

Using the `TableOperation.Retrieve()` will result in calling a special URI made for primary key filtering:

`https://<account-name>.table.core.windows.net/Weathers (PartitionKey='5809844',RowKey='201503151300')`

Our third example is querying for certain selected values from the server. You can do this by using server projection; the following code shows you an example:

```
IQueryable<WeatherEntity> projection = from entity in
table.CreateQuery<WeatherEntity>()
where entity.PartitionKey == "5809844"
select TableQuery.Project(entity, "Temperature");
```

The preceding code selects only the `Temperature` and will not return other properties. When projecting, always make sure the selected property exists in your selection.

 Note that the `PartitionKey`, `RowKey`, `Timestamp`, and `ETag` will always be returned by the server when projecting on certain properties.

Our next example is using LINQ to return the top *n* entities using `Take(n)`; the following code shows how to get top 10 results:

```
IQueryable query = (from weather in table.
CreateQuery<WeatherEntity>()
   where weather.PartitionKey == "5809844"
   select weather).Take(10); //first 10 rows for Seattle
```

Our following example is querying on a property without including the partition key. You can use `where` to query on any property on the table; let's say you want to get all weathers released at a certain year:

```
IQueryable<WeatherEntity> query = from entity in table.
CreateQuery<WeatherEntity>()
   where entity.Humidity == "82"
   select entity;
```

This query will result in a full table scan and is not recommended. It is labeled as an inefficient query and depending on the amount of data you have it may not be performant.

 There are many patterns for structuring and de-normalizing your data in order to avoid inefficient queries. We will be discussing these in the following chapter.

Our last example is performing a type-safe query over a table. Using `DynamicTableEntity` you can invoke schema-free queries. Suppose you have in your table entities that contain properties not defined in your class (like the earlier `Merge` update we performed by adding to dynamic properties `Visibility` and `Pressure`). To achieve this we can do the following:

```
IQueryable<DynamicTableEntity> query = from entity in table.CreateQuer
y<DynamicTableEntity>()
   where entity.Properties["Visibility"].StringValue == "16093"
   select entity;
```

The result will be a collection of `DynamicTableEntities` that contains the full list of the entity's columns in its `Properties` dictionary.

Continuation tokens

Querying large sets of data has some considerations and limitations. A single query has a maximum number of entities per request; it may return up to 1,000 items and its execution time cannot exceed 5 seconds on the server. If the results of a query exceeds these limits, or if a query crosses the partition boundary (a query that crosses to another partition server while searching for the values), the server will include in the response a continuation token to be used to re-query. So, continuation tokens are used as bookmarks to allow queries to resume from where they left off.

By default, the client libraries handle the continuation tokens for you and keep querying the service until all the results are retrieved. But, most of the time, you don't want to retrieve all entities in your table and sometimes you need to do paging. The `TableQuery` class provides an option to use segmented queries by calling the `ExecuteQuerySegmented` method, which returns a partial result and lets you handle continuation tokens as well. The code below shows how this can be achieved:

```
using Microsoft.WindowsAzure.Storage.Table.Queryable;
...
TableQuery<WeatherEntity> query = (from entity in table.
CreateQuery<WeatherEntity>()
select entity).AsTableQuery<WeatherEntity>();

TableContinuationToken continuationToken = null;
List<WeatherEntity> myEntities = new List<WeatherEntity>();

do
{
```

```
    var queryResult = query.ExecuteSegmented(continuationToken);
    continuationToken = queryResult.ContinuationToken;
    myEntities .AddRange(queryResult.Results);


} while (continuationToken != null);
```

In the preceding code, we casted the LINQ query into a `TableQuery` object by using the extension method, `AsTableQuery`, included in the namespace `Microsoft.WindowsAzure.Storage.Table.Queryable`.

We then create a null `TableContinuationToken` which will be used to hold the token returned. As long as the token is not null, we can query for more data.

 The `TableQuery` also exposes an asynchronous `ExecuteSegmentedAsync()` method, which is convenient with the (async/await) methods in C#.

Summary

In this chapter we have discussed the basics of Table storage, which is the key/value NoSQL storage option offered by Azure platform. We have performed basic operations on entities and tables. In the next chapter, we will dive deeper into tables, discussing patterns of structuring data, storing multiple entities in one table, selecting good partition keys, and managing concurrency.

5
Designing Scalable and Performant Tables

In the previous chapter we introduced you to Azure Table storage; we covered the basics of this service and discovered its components and structure. Then we used the Azure Storage Client Library for .NET to operate on tables to create, update, and read entities. While table storage is designed to handle web-scale data, it is very important to know how to make the best of this service. This chapter will focus on the concerns to consider, such as performance, scalability, and cost, while designing your tables.

Things to understand about Azure Table storage

Table storage is built to handle web scale data, allowing intensive and fast read and write transactions. A single account has a target throughput of 20,000 requests per second, while a single table partition can handle up to 2,000 transactions per second.

The service offers a cost-effective storage solution where you only pay for what you use and at a lower cost than on-premises storage options. As of writing this book, the average cost of 1 TB in a table with a local redundancy option is 6.5 cents (US), and 8 cents (US) for a geo-redundant one. Also, Table storage is exposed through a REST API that makes it always available to any client that can make and handle HTTP requests. You can build your own libraries to manage connecting to the REST service, or most probably, you will use one of the open source libraries that are available for most of the development stacks.

Tables are non-relational, which means you cannot have relations and foreign keys between them. They are not an RDBMS; if you want a cloud-hosted relational database you can use the Azure SQL Database. Tables also have some limitations, like the fact that you can have only one index per table, which might affect querying performance.

The table's primary key

The table's primary key consists of the **PartitionKey** and **RowKey** combined; it is the only index for the table and it allows for faster retrieval of data by holding low-level addresses to rows. The rows in a table will always be sorted by the PartitionKey, then the RowKey, and querying a table will also return results sorted by its primary key. Since keys are of string type, it is good to have fixed size keys to ensure good sorting results. For instance, in a query result, an entity with RowKey 123 will appear before an entity with RowKey 2; to fix this it is better to pad out your key to become 002.

 The tables should be designed to be queried using these keys; depending on the size of the table, an ad hoc query could be slow if not using any of the keys. We will examine all types of queries later in this chapter.

The three layer architecture

As a matter of fact, Azure Storage, including blobs, tables and queues, architecture has three fundamental layers:

- The **Frontend (FE)** layer that takes requests, authenticates and authorizes them, and then routes them to the appropriate partition server. The FE layer keeps a partition map, which allows it to know where this data is stored and in what partition.

- The **Partition** layer consists of partition servers and manages the partitioning of objects based on their PartitionKey. In tables, entities belong to partitions that are stored on partition servers; a partition cannot be split and will always be served by the same server. The PL automatically load balances traffic on partitions, such that, if a partition server is serving two hot partitions, it will move one of them into a different lower traffic partition server.

- The **Distributed File System** (DFS) layer is responsible for storing the physical data on disks, and for replicating and distributing the data across multiple servers. All data stored in this layer is accessible from any partition server.

The frontend layer processes a request directed to it by DNS resolution; it performs the necessary authentication and authorization. It then uses the partition key to lookup in its partition map and find the needed partition server. The request then arrives at the Partition layer, and depending on the request type, will send it to one of the DFS servers that holds a replica of the data, if the request is a read operation. If the request is a write or update, the request is sent to the primary DFS server holding the data.

Partitions

A table partition is simply a collection of entities that has the same PartitionKey. Large tables are usually distributed on storage nodes, that is, partition servers, a partition server; can contain one or more partitions. A single partition will never be split across different nodes. If a node is under a heavy load, the service will automatically split the hot partitions to a different node. This is all managed by the service, which can then merge back the partition ranges in case the traffic subsides.

Let us take the example of the weather history database discussed in the previous chapter. In this example, we designed the table to have the `city ID` as the PartitionKey, which defines the partition server:

PartitionKey (city ID)	RowKey (date and time)	...	Partition server (storage node)
...	...		A
276781	201503151300		A
276781	201503151400		A
276781	201503151500		A
...	...		A
...	...		A
5809844	201503151300		B
5809844	201503151400		B
...	...		B
6173331	201503151300		B

The preceding table currently has three logical partitions, which are distributed among two different storage nodes. Assuming partition A has grown big over time, the service will detect that a storage node is not able to serve requests based on SLA targets and it will split the table into two server nodes.

Entity Group Transactions

In the previous chapter, we worked with the **Entity Group Transactions (EGTs)**, which are the only built-in mechanisms for performing batch transaction across multiple entities in a table; thus providing the so-called atomic operations. EGTs only work on entities of the same partition (sharing same partition key), so atomic transactional behavior on entities requires that many entities have the same partition key.

An EGT can operate on a maximum of 100 entities. For improved performance, it is better to batch a single operation per entity in order to avoid any delays.

EGTs are seriously considered when selecting the table's partition key, since they introduce a trade-off that must be studied carefully when designing your tables. Having huge partitions increases the benefits from EGTs performing atomic transactions, thus increasing consistency, but this might limit the scalability of your table since automatic load balancing cannot be done on single partitions.

Choosing between Azure Table and Azure SQL

Table storage and Azure SQL are both cloud-based storage options that benefit from the platform's managed infrastructure, scalability, and high availability. While Azure SQL provides a relational database management system, Table Storage offers NoSQL key-value storage that perfectly suits large amounts of non-relational data. The following are some recommendations for determining which option to choose that best fits the purpose of your application.

If you need to store extremely large amounts of data, you should consider using table storage. A table can hold up to 500 TB of data, while Azure SQL through its best tier, the premium tier, has a maximum database size of 500 GB.

If your data is relational and you do require a relational model to ensure integrity, referential constraints, and primary and foreign keys, you should consider using Azure SQL databases. Table storage is more suitable for tables that do not have complex relationships that requires server-side joins or secondary indexes.

If your application requires spatial data and rich data types, as well as query semantics like joins and aggregation, or requires visualizations and business intelligence reporting using out-of-the-box reporting tools, you should consider using Azure SQL.

The selection between the two should always depend on the architecture and individual needs of your solution, and many times a combination of the two is valid. In summary, if you want to store massive amounts of non-relational data models at a reduced cost, you should consider using Table storage. On the other hand, if your data is relational and requires data processing over schematized data sets, you should consider using Azure SQL.

Table design guidelines

When designing your tables, you should be able to get the most out of the Table storage service in order to achieve and meet your goals. Tables are mostly used for intensive read and write operations, with the ability to scale up as much as needed; thus your design must be tailored to meet your needs and your scenarios.

Things to keep in mind to design **read-efficient** tables:

- When designing for heavy read-querying applications, it is recommended to think about how you will query your data in the most performant way before even thinking how you will be modifying your data.

 For example, the previous weather table design was built around the fact that weather is mostly requested by city and by date.

- As Table storage is relatively cheap, consider the option of storing duplicate copies of your entities with different keys, since the best queries are the ones that specify both the PartitionKey and RowKey, called **point queries**. In our previous example, we can save a duplicate entity with **Temperature** as the RowKey; this will allow users to query on days with same temperature very efficiently.

- Consider normalizing your data to make it as flat as possible; hence there will be no more need for relations.

- Consider having multiple tables for different querying purposes. In our weather sample, we can create a second table with a time-based partition key in order to query heavily on dates and not cities.

Things to keep in mind to design **write-efficient** tables:

- Try not to create hot partitions, allow multiple partitions, so that requests can be spread over multiple servers.

- Do not create a separate table for each entity; you can merge the same entities under the same partition if batch processing is required. For example, in our weather sample you can add an entry for the daily average temperature of each city.

Studying your data

As you already know by now, tables have one single index, which is the combination of both keys. This means that you are unable to add secondary indexes, as you can in the case of relational databases. So, to achieve optimal scalability and query efficiency, you need to analyze your data by determining your partition sizes and understanding how you will query your data.

Partition sizing

More partitions mean better scalability and load balancing. Partition size is the number of entities in one single partition. Understanding your data and choosing your partition key will determine your partition count and size. You might design your table to have only one partition key and on, the other extreme, you might choose the finest level of granularity and insert a unique key for each entity:

- **Choosing a single value for the PartitionKey**: With a low entity count you can perform batch transactions on the entire table. But with a larger number of entities, scaling will be limited and the throughput will be limited to the performance of the same single storage node.

- **Choosing multiple values for the PartitionKey**: The partition size will depend on the entity distribution your data has. Selecting the right partition key value here is very important to gain the best scalability and querying performance.

- **Choosing unique values**: The partition size will be one entity per partition and your table will have many small partitions, which will make the table highly scalable. On the other hand, batch transactions are impossible when using this design.

Querying performance

When designing your tables, it is very important to know what data your application will need. A good question to ask yourself would be, "What queries will my application use to get the data it needs from the table?" You should be able to create a list of queries that you will use, and after that you will need to prioritize them to find the dominant queries that will shape your table design. Since tables are indexed based on their primary keys, selecting these keys should be related to the way your application will query the data.

 Your application may be read intensive, write intensive, or a mix between the two. In general, designing a heavy-read-performant table will lead to an efficient heavy write table.

Let's consider a scenario where you have a website that keeps a record of running race results. Our table `RaceResults` will have a separate row for each race participant in a specific race ,with his timing.

PartitionKey (Race)	RowKey (BiB)	Name	Time
…	…		
Beirut Marathon	7377	Rami Sarieddine	04:09:23
Beirut Marathon	7899	Chukri Soueidi	03:59:26
Beirut Marathon	7966	Mikha Makhoul	03:45:26
Beirut 10 k	8988	Rami Sarieddine	00:36:25
Byblos Half Marathon	1234	Chukri Soueidi	01:46:52
…	…		

The following will show the different types of queries and try to evaluate their performance:

- A point query is a query where you specify both keys, the PartitionKey and RowKey, and return a single entity. This is the most efficient way to query a table with the best performance rating, allowing the table to use its index to retrieve the data. For example, `http://myaccount.table.core.windows.net/Results(PartitionKey="Beirut 10 k" , RowKey="8988")`.

A range query is the second best in terms of performance; it uses the PartitionKey and filters on a range of RowKey values, and might return multiple entities. The PartitionKey will identify what partition contains the data to look for. The search will be limited to finding the ranging entities within the RowKey range requested. For example, `http://myaccount.table.core.windows.net/Results?$filter=PartitionKey eq 'Beirut Marathon ' and RowKey ge '7000' and RowKey lt '8000'`.

- A partition scan is a query that uses the PartitionKey and filters on non-key columns; this will return multiple entities. The partition will be identified, and the search will be focused on that partition to retrieve the desired records. This query is not as performing like the previous ones and it's also affected by the partition size. For example, `http://myaccount.table.core.windows.net/Results?$filter=PartitionKey eq 'Beirut Marathon ' and Name eq 'Chukri Soueidi'`.

- A table scan is a query that does not specify the PartitionKey and will result in a full table scan to get the desired data. Regardless of whether the RowKey has been specified or not, the query will search in every single entity of the table. This is the worst performing query. For example, `http://myaccount.table.core.windows.net/Results?$filter= Name eq 'Chukri Soueidi'`.

Selecting the best PartitionKey

The key selection process might be the trickiest part when it comes to tables. Three things to keep in mind when picking the key:

- **Scalability**: How to be able to distribute data evenly among partitions
- **Efficient queries**: How to avoid frequent large scans
- **Entity Group Transactions**: How to reduce round trips to the server

Your choice of PartitionKey should achieve balance between the above, ensuring scalability, efficient querying and data consistency. Normally, you will find the most suitable property in your entity for distributing your entities into adequate partitions.

Here are some guidelines that will help you select your key:

- If your entity has one key property, use this property as the PartitionKey.
- If your entity has two key properties, use one as PartitionKey and the other as RowKey.

- In many cases you may have more than one dominant query for your entities. You can then insert the same entity multiple times in the table with different RowKeys; this can be managed by your application using EGTs, and is feasible since the cost of data is very low. For instance, in our previous example, we might need to query based on **Name** or based on **BiB** number. You can add two entities in your table as follows:

PartitionKey (Year_Race)	RowKey	Time	Name	Bib	Age
2014_Beirut Marathon	7377	04:09:23	Rami Sarieddine		30
2014_Beirut Marathon	Rami Sarieddine	04:09:23		7377	30

Summary

Azure Table storage is a flexible, NoSQL key-value solution that allows applications to store massive amounts of data and provides automatic partition management. Crafting your tables will affect the success of your solution, so you have to make sure to take scalability and data consistency into consideration.

6
Working with Queues

So far, we have seen two services by Azure Storage: blobs and tables. While the previous services provide persistent storage options, this chapter will introduce you to a different non-persistent storage service, queue storage. Azure Queues provide a reliable system to store messages that need to be consumed afterwards by other tiers. In this chapter, we will explore the characteristics of queues and the way messages are inserted, and then consumed.

The need for queues

Queues are data structures that enable you to queue and de-queue messages into them for later retrieval; they allow you to create a backlog of work. A queue-centric pattern in applications can be simply described as follows: an application uses a queue to keep messages or chunks of data in a quick and ordered way; on the other hand a backend tier(s) of the same or different application is following up on these messages and processing them gradually.

Queues are used in a wide range of applications and they prove to be very effective in addressing many business requirements, such as increasing availability and reliability of systems; reducing latency; load-leveling the workload and deferring processing at peak times; avoiding bottlenecks of IO resources; and distributing communication between heterogeneous platforms.

Increasing the availability and reliability

Applications that are dependent on other services, such as databases or public APIs, need a way to avoid any service interruptions of these external components and not to halt waiting for failed requests. By using Queues, you can loosely couple your components, allowing your app to save its operations without being directly affected by database server availability for instance.

Reducing latency and avoiding IO bottlenecks

Queues can be useful any time you are doing time-consuming work. For example, say you want to create different thumbnails and sizes for any newly uploaded image on your website. It might be unpleasant to keep the user waiting for your background image processing job to run and save the different files on your server. Using queues, you can put this operation in a queue message and send a success "upload" message to your user, and then a worker service will continue the image processing job in the background.

Load leveling

Many applications pass through peak times during which the amount and volume of requests exceeds the capacity that can be handled by its infrastructure. Usually, you can resolve this in two ways: either you purchase additional resources to make sure your infrastructure can handle the worst-case scenarios; or you can simply use queues to keep a backlog of work that needs to be processed later, allowing your application to stay available even during peak times.

Passing messages between Azure web roles and worker roles

Another offering by Azure is Cloud Services; it allows you to deploy applications that can be scaled without the overhead of administration and load balancing. These applications will run on Azure VMs and can be of two types: web roles (web apps) and worker roles (for background processing). In many cases these two roles need to communicate and pass messages between each other and a perfect solution for that would be to use Azure Queues.

The Queue storage structure

Azure Queues offers a simple REST-based service for storing messages that can be accessed and consumed from anywhere via authorized HTTP or HTTPS requests, providing a reliable messaging system for multiple dependent services. It shares the same programming model with the previously discussed tables and blobs, creating a uniform experience for developers.

The service contains the following components:

- **Storage Account**: It provides the namespace and manages access and authorization to all associated queues.

- **Queue**: It stores an unlimited number of messages. Cannot exceed the 500 TB size limit.

- **Message**: It contains a payload of UTF-8 encoded text data. A message can only persist up to seven days in a queue and has a maximum size of 64 KB.

> We have seen in the previous chapter how entities are partitioned in tables, by the partition key, to meet the traffic needs of tables. However, messages in a single queue are grouped into a single partition determined by the queue name and are always served by a single server. Thus, for load balancing, you might consider using multiple queues for highly demanding needs.

Messages are usually stored in JSON format and should always be XML-safe or Base64 encoded. You can use the blob storage service to store large messages while keeping a reference in the queue message.

> For storing files in a message, you can save the binary file in a blob container, then you can insert its URL in the message.

Addressing

Queues are addressable using the following URL pattern:

```
http://<account-name>.queue.core.windows.net/<queue-name>
```

The `<account-name>` placeholder stands for your storage account name and the `<queue-name>` placeholder stands on the name of your queue.

For development using the storage emulator, the URL pattern differs and becomes:

```
http://127.0.0.1:10003/devstorageaccount1/<queue-name>
```

> The `127.0.0.1` IP is the local loopback address for your development machine, and the `devstorageaccount1` is a hardcoded name set by the emulator as the default storage account name.

Naming

When creating queues, there are some naming rules to follow:

- **Queue**: A queue name must be unique within its storage account, and range from 3 to 63 characters long. It can only contain alphanumeric characters or non-consecutive dash (-) characters and cannot begin or end with a dash, nor start with a number. All letters in a queue name must be lowercase.

- **Metadata**: A queue can have its own metadata stored with it as name-value properties. Property names are case-insensitive and must adhere to the C# identifiers naming rules; they must also be unique per queue.

Service Bus Queues

The Azure platform currently offers two different queuing services: Azure Queues and Service Bus Queues. Service Bus is a broader type of messaging service that provides a number of additional capabilities over the storage queues.

In summary, Service Bus provides four different communication mechanisms that are designed to integrate applications or hybrid application components. These entities are Queues, Topics, Relays, and Event Hubs. Service Bus Queues are brokers that store messages; Topics are queues that offer a pub/sub mechanism where multiple applications subscribe to a queue and filter their messages based on certain topics; Relays provide bidirectional direct communication between two separate applications that, for example, might be both residing on premises; Event Hub is an event processing service for large scale data intake.

Choosing between Service Bus Queues and Azure Queues depends on multiple factors that should be considered based on the individual requirements of your application. Service Bus Queues offers more features but with a higher overhead on developers. In this chapter, we will be only focusing on Azure Queues since it is part of the Azure Storage infrastructure.

For a full comparison between these two queue services, check the MSDN article *Azure Queues and Service Bus Queues - Compared and Contrasted*:

```
https://msdn.microsoft.com/en-us/library/azure/
hh767287.aspx
```

Using the queue storage from .NET

The Azure Storage Client Library for .NET has all the classes and methods needed to work with queues programmatically. After creating a storage account, and getting the appropriate access keys (both discussed in earlier chapters), we now have everything it takes to utilize the storage service using the .NET framework.

For the simplicity of our code samples, we will be using a C# **Console Application** template. To create an empty console application open Visual Studio and navigate to **New Project** | **Templates** | **Visual C#** | **Console Application**.

By default, the application will not include the storage client library, so we need to add it using the package manager by typing `Install-Package WindowsAzure.Storage`. This will download and install the library along with all dependencies required.

> You can navigate through the library by expanding **References** in **Solution Explorer** in Visual Studio and right-click **Microsoft. WindowsAzure.Storage** and selecting **View** in **Object Browser**. This will show you the whole library classes and methods.

After getting the storage library, we need to create the connection string by providing the storage account name and access key. The connection string will look like this:

```
    <appSettings>
  <add key="StorageConnectionString"
       value="DefaultEndpointsProtocol=https;
       AccountName=account name;AccountKey=access key/>
  </appSettings>
```

In `program.cs` we need to reference the following libraries:

```
using System.Configuration; // reference to System.Configuration
should be added to the project
using Microsoft.WindowsAzure.Storage;
using Microsoft.WindowsAzure.Storage.Queue;
```

> Alternatively, you can use the Azure Cloud Service project template to create services that run on Azure. A cloud service can contain web roles and worker roles. Typically, Azure Queues is filled by web roles (for example, ASP.NET application) and then processed by worker roles (Windows Service), which is always querying the queue for new messages to handle.

Creating our first queue

Using the connection string defined in the `App.config` file, we will proceed to create a `CloudStorageAccount` object. This object represents the storage account where the queue will be created along with all the security details and the endpoint definitions. After that we need to initialize a `CloudQueueClient` object, which represents a frontage for dealing with queues. Using that `CloudQueueClient` object we can get a queue reference and then call the `queue.CreateIfNotExists()` method that will actually call the table REST API under the hood to create a queue and return a `True` Boolean value. If there exists a queue with the same name or the queue name doesn't follow queue naming rules, the method will return `false`.

The following is the code to do that:

```
string connectionString = ConfigurationManager.AppSettings["StorageCon
nectionString"];
            CloudStorageAccount storageAccount = CloudStorageAccount.
Parse(connectionString);

            CloudQueueClient queueClient = storageAccount.
CreateCloudQueueClient();
            CloudQueue queue = queueClient.GetQueueReference("firstqu
eue");
            bool b = queue.CreateIfNotExists();
```

Inserting a message in the queue

After creating a new queue, we will now insert our first message into it. In order to do that, we need to use the `CloudQueueMessage` class to create a message wrapper object then pass it to `CloudQueue:AddMessage` method:

```
            CloudQueueMessage message = new CloudQueueMessage("First
Task !");
        queue.AddMessage(message);
```

The `CloudQueueMessage` class has three constructors that you can use in order to initialize it: the first one takes one parameter that should be a byte array; the second one accepts also a single parameter but of type string, like the one we used above; and the third one takes two string parameters that should specify a given message ID and pop receipt (we will talk about these in later sections).

The table below shows two additional parameters that can be passed to the `AddMessage` method while saving a message to the queue:

Parameter	Data type	Description
timeToLive	TimeSpan	Specifies the amount of time the message will persist in the queue before it gets automatically purged from the server. The value cannot exceed the default and maximum message life (seven days).
initialVisibilityDelay	TimeSpan	Specifies the interval of time from insertion time during which the message will be invisible. If null then the message will be visible immediately.

Now to demonstrate these extra parameters, the code sample below will set the message's `timeToLive` to four days and `initialVisibilityDelay` to 30 seconds:

```
TimeSpan timeToLive = TimeSpan.FromDays(4); // cannot
    exceed 7 days
TimeSpan initialVisibilityDelay =
    TimeSpan.FromSeconds(30);

queue.AddMessage(message, timeToLive,
    initialVisibilityDelay);
```

Handling large messages

As we mentioned before, the maximum size of a queue message cannot exceed 64 KB. For instance, let's say your application has the scenario that we have seen before where a user uploads an image to your app that is following a queue centric pattern and you wish to create different thumbnails for it. At first glance, the messages (images in this case) appear to have sizes that exceed the maximum limit for messages. We can get around this problem by uploading the images to a blob container and only saving a reference for them in the queue messages. The background agent that is responsible for creating these thumbnails will then retrieve the message from queue, reference the blobs and then get the image.

The following is some sample code:

```
CloudBlobClient blobClient =
  storageAccount.CreateCloudBlobClient();
     CloudBlobContainer blobContainer =
       blobClient.GetContainerReference("uploads");
     blobContainer.CreateIfNotExists();

     using (var file = new
     FileStream(@"D:\uploads\myphoto.jpg", FileMode.Open))
{
     string blobId = Guid.NewGuid().ToString();
     CloudBlockBlob blob =
       blobContainer.GetBlockBlobReference(blobId);
     blob.UploadFromStream(file);
}

     queue.AddMessage(new CloudQueueMessage(blobId));
```

The code we used to create the blob and blob container was fully covered in *Chapter 3, Working with Blobs*.

Retrieving the next message

To consume the stored messages, each time your app needs to de-queue the first next messages from the queue; to do this we will use the `queue.GetMessage()` method. Once a message is retrieved, it will be invisible for any other services or apps trying to get messages from the same queue. By default, you will only have 30 seconds to process the message and delete it, during which it will be invisible to others. This is known as visibility timeout.

After successfully processing the message, you will have to delete it from the queue using the `DeleteMessage` method. Following is an example of how to do that:

```
CloudQueueMessage frontMessage = queue.GetMessage();

     //Do work here: process the message in less than 30
seconds, and then delete the message

     queue.DeleteMessage(frontMessage);
```

To control the visibility timeout, you can manually set the `visibilityTimeout` parameter while getting a message just like the following:

```
CloudQueueMessage frontMessage =
    queue.GetMessage(TimeSpan.FromSeconds(90));
//This will keep the message invisible
    in the queue, giving you more time
    to process the request.
```

The queue service returns additional data along with each message that is filled inside the returned `CloudQueueMessage` object as properties. The table below lists the most important of these:

Property	Data type	Description
InsertionTime	DateTimeOffset	The time that the message was added to the queue.
ExpirationTime	DateTimeOffset	The time that the message expires.
DequeueCount	Integer	The number of time the message has been retrieved. If the dequeuer count is high, this might be an indicator that something is wrong with the message and that it might be a poison message. (To be discussed later in this chapter).
TimeNextVisible	DateTimeOffset	The time the message will be visible in the queue again. This is calculated by adding the `visibilityTimeout` to time the message was retrieved.
PopReceipt	String	A token calculated by the service and given to each consumer retrieving the message. The owner of the last PopReceipt issued is the only one who is able to edit or delete the message.

The `PopReceipt` is used to prove the current ownership of the message. It will become invalid if the owner failed to process the message within the allowed time and other consumer de-queued the same message. The holder of the latest receipt is the only one eligible to edit or delete the message.

Getting more messages

For many reasons, you might prefer to sometimes retrieve a batch of messages in a single GET request. By using the GetMessages method you are able to retrieve a variable number of queue messages, up to 32. The return type of the method will be an IEnumerable<CloudQueueMessage> that can be iterated using a foreach loop:

```
foreach (CloudQueueMessage mess in
    queue.GetMessages(10, TimeSpan.FromMinutes(2)))
        {
            // Process the message
            string message = mess.AsString;
            queue.DeleteMessage(mess);
        }
```

The dequeueCount and poison messages

From time to time, a message may not be processed successfully by your consuming service which will make it reappear after a certain period. This might be due to several reasons, such as an error in the stored data or maybe a programming defect in your consuming job. The dequeueCount property retrieved with every message can help us discover poison messages. It is good practice to check this number with every GET message request. If the dequeueCount is greater than three, you might want to flag it as a poisoned message and log it somewhere else such as a separate queue for later handling. The code below demonstrates this:

```
    CloudQueueMessage message = queue.GetMessage();
if (message.DequeueCount >= 3)
        {
            // handle the poison the message
            // move it to a special queue for later management
    }
```

Peeking messages

Queues provide a method to read the next message without de-queuing it. This might be useful if you want to sneak peek on the next message during development or debugging time. This can be done using the PeekMessage method:

```
    CloudQueueMessage peekedMessage = queue.PeekMessage();
```

Editing queue messages

Though it is not commonly used, it is possible to retrieve a message and update its content and then push it back to the queue. This might be useful in the case of a multi-step workflow, where you are saving the current step. Or you might need to change the visibility timeout for a message:

```
message.SetMessageContent("Step:1");
        queue.UpdateMessage(message,
            TimeSpan.FromSeconds(120),
            MessageUpdateFields.Content | MessageUpdateFields.
Visibility);
```

The code above shows how to use the `SetMessageContent` to change the content of a retrieved message then uses the `UpdateMessage` to push the content changes and the visibility timeout update, specifying that both have been updated.

Setting metadata for the queue

Adding additional properties to your queue is possible by setting metadata name/value properties for it. You might, for instance, wish to add the date the queue was created, or the name of the developer or user that created this queue. The following code shows you how to do this:

```
queue.Metadata.Add("CreationDate", DateTime.Now.ToString());
        queue.Metadata.Add("Creator", "John Doe");

        queue.SetMetadata();
```

To get all the `Metadata` properties, you need to explicitly call the `FetchAttributes` method in order for the `Metadata` property to be populated from the server. The data will be filled in a `Dictionary` object:

```
queue.FetchAttributes();
IDictionary<string, string> metadata = queue.Metadata;
```

Getting the queue length and metadata

You can query a queue for the number of messages it contains. This is useful for monitoring your queues and the performance of the background services consuming it.

To do that you need to fetch the queue's attributes by calling the FetchAttributes method on the queue, which will fill the ApproximateMessageCount:

```
queue.FetchAttributes();
int? messagecount = queue.ApproximateMessageCount;
```

Deleting queues

You can delete a created queue by calling the Delete method of the queue. Needless to say, this will delete all the messages contained in it. The following is the simple command to do it:

```
queue.Delete();
```

Summary

In this chapter we covered the basics for the Azure Queue service, we learned how to create a queue and how to enqueue and de-queue it with messages as well as how to handle large messages by using a hybrid solution between the blob service and queue service. In the next chapter, we will dig into file storage, which offers shared storage for applications using the common standard **Server Message Block (SMB)** protocol.

7

Working with the Azure File Service

In this chapter, we will be introducing the Azure File service by Azure Storage. This service allows you to create file shares between multiple Azure VMs using the SMB 2.1 protocol. The shares can then be accessed by applications using standard Windows File APIs or via Files REST API (part of the Storage REST APIs), making persistent data sharing very easy among various **Infrastructure as a Service (IaaS)** and **Platform as a Service (PaaS)** Azure components. The Azure File service is built on the same technology as blobs, tables, and queues; thus, it leverages the existing availability, durability, scalability, and geo-redundancy that are built into the platform.

Where are Azure Files used?

The Azure File offering complements the storage services by allowing on-premises legacy applications to be lifted and shifted to the cloud. Cloud applications can easily share files between virtual machines using standard and familiar APIs such as **ReadFile** and **WriteFile**.

Many distributed applications have a common pattern of storing configuration files in centralized locations where they can be used by several machines. Such files can be stored via Azure File shares and accessed uniformly; the same files can also be accessed via REST APIs, making them available to the internet via authenticated calls. So, imagine the variety of hybrid scenarios here.

In another scenario, IT administrators and developers might want to share frequently used tools and utilities needed for administering VMs and cloud services. Using Azure Files, this can be done without the cumbersome effort of distributing these files manually. You may even want to share documents and notebooks between teams. Also, you can use file shares for storing diagnostic data, such as logs and crash dumps, in centralized locations.

> The **Server Message Block** (**SMB**) protocol, which the Azure File service uses to expose its files, is an application layer protocol used to provide access to files and other miscellaneous communications between network nodes. It is the most used file share protocol on premises today. With Azure File storage you can leverage the Azure's SMB (IaaS), eliminating the need to rewrite SMB client applications.

The File storage structure

The service consists of the following parts that can be dealt with as separate resources:

- **Storage account**: It provides the namespace, and it manages access and authorization for all associated shares..

- **Share**: It is the container for directories and files. It can contain up to 5 TB of data. Multiple shares can be created under the same storage account, providing the storage capacity quota, which is a maximum of 500 TB, is not exceeded.

- **Directory**: It is an optional way of containing files or other sub-directories.

- **File**: It is a single file that can be up to 1 TB in size.

- **URL**: It provides an endpoint for exposing the above resources, which can be accessed by the REST API.

The URL pattern for accessing a file is:

```
https://<storage-account>.file.core.windows.net/<share>/
<directory>/<file>
```

Using Azure Files

In the following sections, we will discuss the ways to create and use file shares; add directories to it; list, upload, and download files to those directories. We will understand how to perform the same operations using Azure PowerShell and then by using the .NET Storage Client Library. We will start with PowerShell, which is preferred by IT administrators since it allows the automation of most of their tasks.

 At the time of writing this book, Azure File is still in preview, so in order to use the service you will need to sign up for it on the Microsoft Azure Preview Portal, by navigating to **Preview Features** and selecting **Azure File for trial**. After requesting the feature, you will receive an email confirming the activation of your subscription for the Microsoft Azure File. Using storage accounts that have been created prior to requesting the feature will not work; instead you will need to create a new storage account in order to get your file share endpoints provisioned.

Using PowerShell with Azure Files

With Azure PowerShell, you can create and manage file shares. The Azure PowerShell leverages the Azure Service Management REST API to operate on the storage service. With it you can mount shares to your file system, provided that it supports the SMB 2.1 protocol. But before we discuss how to perform these various tasks, let us briefly describe PowerShell.

Getting familiar with Azure PowerShell

PowerShell is a powerful tool that allows you to access and use remote and local resources. PowerShell is used by IT administrators and developers for task automation and configuration management. It is a complete framework that consists of two parts: the command-line shell (the interface) and its scripting language.

 At the heart of its scripting language are **cmdlets**. They are predefined self-descriptive commands that implement specific functions and provide higher scripting abilities.

Azure PowerShell is a submodule that is built to support all Azure-specific functionalities. Combining **cmdlets**, you can prepare script files (.ps1 files) to be run whenever needed, making automation possible for the different facets of Azure Storage without needing to manually perform the same operations every time on the portal.

There are a plenty of storage commands included in the Azure service management **cmdlets** and they are very well documented on MSDN. Refer to:

https://msdn.microsoft.com/en-us/library/dn806401.aspx

When using PowerShell, you will need to authenticate with your storage subscription; this can be done either by using management certificates or by authenticating via Azure Active Directory.

For more documentation on how to install and configure Azure PowerShell you can use the following link:

https://azure.microsoft.com/en-us/documentation/articles/powershell-install-configure/

 I, personally, advise using the PowerShell **Integrated Scripting Environment** (ISE); it is a more intuitive environment that adds to the scripting experience, with features such as IntelliSense, syntax-coloring, visual debugging, and much more.

Creating a file share

After setting up Azure PowerShell, you need to connect to the storage account and create a storage account context, supplying the storage account name and key (both can be retrieved from the portal).

To create the context in the PowerShell console, we will use the New-AzureStorageContext cmdlet:

```
$context = New-AzureStorageContext <account-name> <account-key>
```

Next, the New-AzureStorageShare cmdlet can be used to create a new share using the above account context. In the following code we will create a new file share named shareddocs:

```
$share = New-AzureStorageShare shareddocs -Context $context
```

Share names must be a valid DNS name; they can contain only numbers or letters, with the dash (-) character allowed in between characters; they are always lower case, ranging from 3 to 63 characters long.

Creating directories and subdirectories

In order to create a directory in a share, we use the `New-AzureStorageDirectory` cmdlet as shown in the following command:

```
New-AzureStorageDirectory -Share $share -Path ApplicationFiles
```

In the preceding command, the created directory is named `ApplicationFiles`. To create a subdirectory named `GeneralFiles`, you execute the following cmdlet:

```
New-AzureStorageDirectory -Share $share -Path ApplicationFiles/
GeneralFiles
```

Uploading the first file

In order to populate the created file share, you need to use the `Set-AzureStorageFileContent` cmdlet, which uploads the contents of a local file to the specified share and path (directory):

```
Set-AzureStorageFileContent -Share $share -Source C:\temp\readme.txt
-Path ApplicationFiles
```

The preceding command uploads a local file named `readme.txt` to the directory `ApplicationFiles` in the `shareddocs` file share.

Downloading a file

To download a file uploaded to the file share, you can use the `Get-AzureStorageFileContent` cmdlet, which downloads the file and then saves it to the specified destination:

```
Get-AzureStorageFileContent -Share $share -Path ApplicationFiles/readme.
txt -Destination C:\downloads.
```

The preceding command downloads a `readme.txt` file from the cloud to the local machine running the command.

Listing files

The Get-AzureStorageFile cmdlet is used to list all directories and files on a specified path. You can add the IsDirectory pipeline property to distinguish between folders and files. The following command lists the contents of the specified directory in the -Path argument:

```
Get-AzureStorageFile -Share $share -Path ApplicationFiles
```

Removing files

To delete a file, you can use the Remove-AzureStorageFile cmdlet. The command below will delete the file readme.txt:

```
Remove-AzureStorageFile -Share $share -Path ApplicationFiles/readme.txt
```

File Shares via the SMB 2.1 protocol

Azure file shares can be accessed using the SMB 2.1 protocol by multiple VMs at the same time. To demonstrate this, we will mount a previously created file share from a virtual machine. This will allow the share to appear on the file system with its assigned letter as a mapped network drive.

Using the Windows Command Prompt or PowerShell, you can execute the net use command to mount the file share using the following syntax:

```
net use <drive-letter>: \\<storage-account-name>.file.core.windows.
net\<share-name> /u:<storage-account-name> <storage-account-key>
```

After running the command, you will see that a share has been added below your mapped drives, taking the drive-letter you assigned to it. You may use the **File Explorer** to add and delete files and directories; you may also use the command prompt to issue standard file commands. The files can be accessed programmatically by running an app that uses the .NET System.IO namespace (or any other file I/O API) to read, write, and manage the files and directories.

Keep in mind that you can only mount a share from a virtual machine that is running in the same region as your storage account. Otherwise, you will get system error number 64 saying: The specified network name is no longer available. In order to be able to map in different regions, you will need to run **WebDav** on your virtual machine.

Persisting connections to shares

By default, a mounted drive will not be persisted after a machine reboot since the credentials used to create the drive will not be preserved. In order to store them, you need to execute the `cmdkey add` command. The `cmdkey` command allows administrators to create, list, and delete usernames with their passwords for a computer.

Using the command prompt on the virtual machine, you can run the following command to save the account's credentials:

```
cmdkey /add:<account-name>.file.core.windows.net /user:<account-name> /
pass:<account-key>
```

You can then mount a persisted file share that will remain after reboots or shutdowns by simply running the previous command without any credentials:

```
net use <drive-letter>: \\<storage-account-name>.file.core.windows.
net\<share-name>
```

> The Azure File service does not support every feature of the SMB 2.1 protocol, though it supports the features required by the majority of applications. These unsupported features include some that are not applicable to the cloud. Examples of unsupported features are: extended attributes, alternate data streams, named pipes, and so on. For the full list refer to:
>
> https://msdn.microsoft.com/en-us/library/azure/dn744326.aspx

Mounting shares from Linux

If you have a Linux VM, you can still mount an Azure File share to its file system. First, you will have to install any tool that allows mounting SMB shares on Linux, like **cifs-utils**.

> To get the tool, run the following command:
> `sudo apt-get install cifs-utils`

Then you will need to create a directory where you will mount the share, using the following command:

```
mkdir /azure-file-share
```

After that, you can run the following command to mount the Azure File share:

```
sudo mount -t cifs //<storage-account-name>.file.core.windows.net/<share-
name> ./azure-file-share  -o  vers=2.1, username=<storage-account-name>,
password=<storage-account-key>, dir_mode=0777, file_mode=0777
```

File Shares via the Storage Client Library

Mounting shares through PowerShell or SMB requires certain permissions on virtual machines. However, utilizing the service from external places, like from apps, will require accessing the service through its REST APIs. The APIs make the service available to any HTTP-enabled app.

In the following sections, we will operate on file shares using C# in a simple console application. To create a console application open Visual Studio and navigate to **New Project | Templates | Visual C# | Console Application**.

By default, the application does not have a reference to the storage client library, so we need to add it, using the **Package Manager**, by typing `Install-Package WindowsAzure.Storage`. This will download and install the library along with all other dependencies required.

 You can navigate through the library by expanding **References** in Solution Explorer in Visual Studio, and right-clicking on **Microsoft. WindowsAzure.Storage** and selecting **View in Object Browser**. This will show you the complete library classes and methods.

After getting the storage libraries, we need to create the connection string by providing the account name and access key. The connection string will look like this:

```
<appSettings>
   <add key="StorageConnectionString"           value="DefaultEndp
ointsProtocol=https;AccountName=account name;AccountKey=access key/>
   </appSettings>
```

In `program.cs` we also need to reference the following libraries:

```
using System.Configuration;  // reference to System.Configuration

should be added to the project
using Microsoft.WindowsAzure.Storage;
using Microsoft.WindowsAzure.Storage.File;
```

Creating our share

We will now use a set of classes to create a share programmatically. The classes involved are `CloudStorageAccount`, `CloudFileClient`, and `CloudFileShare`. The following code will reference those classes, respectively, to create the share using the `CreateIfNotExists` method, which will return a Boolean of `True`, indicating that the share was newly created, or `False`, indicating that the share already exists.

The following is the code to do this:

```
    string connectionString = ConfigurationManager.AppSettings["StorageC
onnectionString"];
            CloudStorageAccount storageAccount = CloudStorageAccount.
Parse(connectionString);
  CloudFileClient cloudFileClient = storageAccount.
CreateCloudFileClient();
            CloudFileShare share = cloudFileClient.
GetShareReference("myshare");
            share.CreateIfNotExists();
```

Creating a directory

In order to create a directory, in a file share, you need to use the `CloudFileDirectory` class. You will also have to reference the share's root directory so that you create your directory inside it. This can be done by the following code:

```
CloudFileDirectory rootDir = share.GetRootDirectoryReference();
    rootDir.CreateIfNotExists();
```

We will now create a `Settings` folder in the root directory:

```
    CloudFileDirectory myDir = rootDir.GetDirectoryReference("Settin
gs");
    sampleDir.CreateIfNotExists();
```

Uploading and downloading files

The `CloudFile` class represents a file in the Azure File service. In the following code we will upload a file from our local disk:

```
    CloudFile uploadFile = myDir.GetFileReference("help.txt");
    uploadFile.UploadFromFile(@"C:\temp\help.txt", System.IO.FileMode.
Open);
```

In the first statement, we created a cloud file reference called `help.txt`. The second statement will get a local file from your disk and upload it to the previously initialized cloud file. You can also upload a byte array, a stream, or plain text. These are the available upload methods: `UploadFromByteArray`, `UploadFromByteArrayAsync`, `UploadFromFile`, `UploadFromFileAsync`, `UploadFromStream`, `UploadFromStreamAsync`, `UploadText`, and `UploadTextAsync`.

 Each function has an *async* overload to facilitate asynchronous programming.

To download the uploaded file, we will now do the same steps but calling the `DownloadToFile` method:

```
CloudFile downloadedFile = myDir.GetFileReference("help.txt");
downloadedFile.DownloadToFile(@"C:\temp\help-online.txt",
FileMode.Create);
```

You also have many flavors for a download; basically, the same options as for the upload.

Using AzCopy

AzCopy is a free command-line tool that is offered by Microsoft. It allows you to easily copy and transfer data from and to Azure storage. It is designed for high performance transfers, with some really good features like verbose logging and progress monitor. AzCopy allows users to select items by specifying patterns, like wildcards or prefixes, to identify the needed files for upload or download. It currently supports blobs, files, and table storage.

After installing the software, in order to upload a set of files in a local directory to your Azure File share, you can run the following command in the AzCopy command-line console:

```
AzCopy /Source:C:\temp /Dest:https://<account-name>.file.core.windows.
net/<share-name>/ /DestKey:<account-key>  /Pattern:set* /S
```

The preceding command will recursively upload all files specified in the source folder with a name matching the pattern `set*` for our file share.

To download the file you would use the following command:

```
AzCopy /Source:https://< account-name>.file.core.windows.net/<share-
name>/ /Dest:C:\temp /SourceKey:< account-key>    /Pattern:help.txt
```

> To download AzCopy, use the following link:
> `http://aka.ms/downloadazcopy`.

Summary

Azure Files adds to the wide-ranging possibilities of Microsoft Azure. It is something many consumers have been asking for in order to migrate their hybrid and legacy applications from being on premises to the cloud. With the Azure blob, disks, and files, you really have several ways to maintain and store data in the cloud. Our next, final, chapter will be on monitoring features and error handling.

8
Transient Fault Handling and Analytics

The following chapter will equip you with the easy means to help you identify, fix, and survive failures. There are two types of failures that may occur in apps using cloud services: enduring failures which are those that require handling and intervention either from administrators or programs, and transient errors which are those that are moments of service interruptions such as network issues. By understanding the monitoring and telemetry tools offered by Azure, you will be able to detect errors and perform a deep root-cause analysis on different issues.

Transient fault handling

When using cloud services, a good thing to keep in mind is that infrastructure is shared among multiple tenants. The Azure platform is designed to support millions of other users, and each service has certain threshold values. A queue, for instance, cannot process more than 2000 messages per second.

Errors that occur due to temporary reasons, such as network issues, connection failures, intermittent service, and infrastructure level faults or even service throttling, are called **transient faults**. These errors are impermanent and can be identified by the HTTP status that is returned with a failed response. Your application must be designed to identify and handle these faults; this can be done by implementing retry policies, which simply retry the same requests again multiple times and sometimes with a delay.

Fortunately, most client libraries implement a certain retry policy functionality. The .NET library implements it through the `Microsoft.WindowsAzure.Storage.RetryPolicies` namespace, which offers three different types:

- **Exponential retry**: It retries the request after an exponential back-off period for a specified number of times. For example, the first retry might be after 2 seconds, the second retry after 4 seconds, and the third after 8 seconds.

- **Linear Retry**: It retries the request after a fixed interval of time for a specified number of times.

- **No Retry**: It represents a retry policy that does not perform any retries.

If the specified number of retires is reached, the retry policy will give up and throw an exception to be handled by the application.

> You can create your own custom retry policy class by implementing the `IRetryPolicy` interface.

The following code will show you how to implement an exponential retry policy for blob operations using C#:

```
CloudBlobClient blobClient = storageAccount.CreateCloudBlobClient();
IRetryPolicy exponentialRetryPolicy = new ExponentialRetry(TimeSpan.
FromSeconds(2), 10);
blobClient.DefaultRequestOptions.RetryPolicy = exponentialRetryPolicy;
```

In the preceding code, we created an `ExponentialRetry` class, and gave it a back-off period of 2 seconds and a maximum number of 10 retries. For a linear retry policy you can do the following:

```
IRetryPolicy linearRetryPolicy = new LinearRetry(TimeSpan.
FromSeconds(2), 10);
```

> A good alternative to the built-in retry policies offered by the Storage Client Library is the **Transient Fault Handling Application Block**, which is part of the **Enterprise Library 5.0 for Windows Azure**. The advantage of using Topaz is that in addition to storage services it supports, Azure SQL, service bus, and the caching service. Thus, you can create a unified retry policy for the different components of your application.

Storage Analytics

Storage Analytics is a built-in monitoring solution for Azure Storage that is used for analyzing usage trends, and diagnosing issues by performing logging and collecting of metrics on request.

The collected data from transactions falls under two types: **Storage Analytics Metrics** and **Storage Analytics Logging**:

- **Metrics** calculates aggregated data for bandwidth usage, errors, server processing time, latencies, and so on, in addition to capacity monitors for blobs

- **Request logging** provides traces for authenticated and anonymous requests made on the storage service

By default, when you create a storage account, and to avoid any additional storage costs, the storage analytics will be disabled. In order to enable it, the easiest way is to navigate to the portal and then to the storage account where you can enable it for blobs, tables, and queues separately, excluding the file service which currently doesn't support storage analytics. You can also enable the analytics using PowerShell commands or programmatically using the storage client library.

The data for request logging will be stored in a hidden blob named `$logs`; and for metrics the data is stored in predefined tables with a retention period after which they will be automatically deleted. Accessing this data can be done the same way we access blobs and tables. The analytics data can be read and deleted only, you cannot add into it. There is also a 20 GB limit that the storage analytics data cannot exceed; in the case that the quota is reached, no new data will be appended until you delete some of the existing data.

A closer look at metrics

Storage Analytics Metrics calculates and collects aggregates and statistics on two things: transactions and blob capacity. When enabling the monitoring, you need to specify the level of metrics collection and the data retention policy. Four main parameters should be defined when setting monitoring:

- **Metrics type**: It is by hour or by minute
- **Service type**: It specifies which service, such as blob, queue, or table

- **Metrics level**: It can have three values:
  - ° None, equivalent to off
  - ° Service level (minimal), which stores aggregate statistics for all requests
  - ° API level (verbose), which stores aggregated records for every operation type made
- **Retention period**: It specifies how long (up to 365 days) the metrics data will be stored

As mentioned earlier, you can enable metrics either from the Azure Management Portal, using PowerShell cmdlets, or programmatically using built-in functions in the Storage Client Library you are using. When enabled, tables will be generated by Azure to store the output of metrics collection.

These well-known tables will be stored in the same place as your own created tables. They will be hidden and will not appear in any listing request to the Table storage service; you will have to access them directly by their names. Therefore, the following is the set of the metrics-containing tables:

Table name	Metrics type	Service
$MetricsHourPrimaryTransactionsBlob	Hourly	Blob
$MetricsHourPrimaryTransactionsTable	Hourly	Table
$MetricsHourPrimaryTransactionsQueue	Hourly	Queue
$MetricsMinutePrimaryTransactionsBlob	Minutes	Blob
$MetricsMinutePrimaryTransactionsTable	Minutes	Table
$MetricsMinutePrimaryTransactionsQueue	Minutes	Queue
$MetricsCapacityBlob	Capacity	Blob

You can access these tables through the Table service APIs, via the namespace of your storage account using the following URI pattern, you can also use any Storage Client Library to do so:

```
https://<accountname>.table.core.windows.net/Tables("Table-Name")
```

Transaction metrics

Transaction metrics can store data by hour or by minute for each storage service. Each service generates two kinds of summaries: the service-level summary, which aggregates data for the whole and, the API-level summary, which stores aggregates for a specific API call, like `CreateContainer`.

The following is a subset of the most important columns that are collected and stored:

- `Time (PartitionKey)`: It represents the start hour or minute in UTC for the metrics, in the format of *YYYYMMddThhmm* and is the PartitionKey of the record.

  Example: 20140809T0800

- `AccessType and TransactionType (RowKey)`: It is a concatenation of two values in format `AccessType; TransactionType` that forms the `RowKey` of the record.

  `AccessType` can have two values:

    ○ *user* for user requests, including authenticated, anonymous, and Shared Access Signature requests

    ○ *system* for operations performed by Storage Analytics itself

  `TransactionType` can also have two values:

    ○ *all* for service-level aggregates

    ○ *api-name* for api-level aggregates

  Example: user; ListBlobs

- `TotalRequests`: It is the sum total of all requests made to the storage service or specific API operation.

- `TotalBillableRequests`: It is the number of all billable requests (some requests are not billable will be discussed later).

- `TotalIngress`: It is the amount of bytes entering the service or operation.

- `TotalEgress`: It is the amount of bytes exiting the service or operation.

- `Availability`: It is the percentage availability of the service or operation. This is calculated by dividing the `TotalBillableRequests` by the `TotalRequests`.

- `AverageE2ELatency`: It is the average end-to-end latency of successful requests, in milliseconds. It includes the network latency in addition to the time needed by the server to produce the response and send it.

- `AverageServerLatency`: It is the time needed in milliseconds for the server to process a request.

- `PercentSuccess`: It is the percentage of successful requests

 For the full schema you can check out the MSDN document *Storage Analytics Metrics Table Schema* at `https://msdn.microsoft.com/en-us/library/azure/hh343264.aspx`.

Capacity metrics

Capacity metrics are currently available for blobs and have a different schema from transaction metrics. They are stored in a table named `$MetricsCapacityBlob`, which has only two records per day. One record summarizes all user blobs and the other summarizes the `$logs` container that holds the logging information mentioned earlier.

This table has only three important counts, which are:

- `Capacity`: It is the amount of bytes used by all containers and blobs in the service

- `ContainerCount`: It gives the number of blob containers in the account

- `ObjectCount`: It is the number of committed and uncommitted block or page blobs in the account

A closer look at logging

Logging saves detailed information on every single request made to blobs, tables, and queues. You can choose the types of requests you want to log, such as read, write, and delete. You can also choose how much time the log data will be retained for by specifying the retention days setting.

The logs are stored in block blobs inside the storage account itself; they are contained in a hidden container named `$logs`.

 The $ sign before the container's names makes it hidden and thus it will not show in listing operations unless it was specified directly by its name.

The URI pattern for accessing the log files is as follows:

```
https://<account-name>.blob.core.windows.net/$logs/<service-name>/
YYYY/MM/DD/hhmm/<counter>.log
```

The physical files that contain these logs have additional metadata that can be very useful for identifying which files you are interested in. These metadata attributes are:

- `LogType` is a combination of the types of operations in a particular file, such as write, read, and delete
- `StartTime` specifies the time of first entry in the file
- `EndTime` specifies the time of the last entry in the file
- `LogVersion` specifies the log format which we will discuss shortly

The log format

The log files contain entries that have a specific unified format for all types of requests. The fields are semicolon (`;`) separated, except for the field in the entry, which has the `\n` to mark the end of the entry.

An entry will contain many fields, of which a few are listed:

- Transaction start time
- REST operation type
- Transaction status
- HTTP status
- E2E latency
- Server latency
- Authentication type
- Accessing account
- Service type
- Request URL
- Operation #
- User IP

 For full documentation, you can refer to MSDN article *Storage Analytics Log Format* at `https://msdn.microsoft.com/en-us/library/azure/hh343259.aspx`.

Analyzing the Storage Analytics data

Storage Analytics offers the ability to track and analyze the usage of your storage services. By analyzing the data, you should be able to improve the overall performance and quality of your applications.

Metrics data is usually analyzed to gain an insight on the service availability, the success percentages of requests, and the total number of requests made on the different services. Using the portal, you can also configure e-mail alerts to be notified when specific metrics reach certain values.

With the logging data, you have a complete trace of all requests and responses. You can, for example, find the exact number of requests coming from a certain range of IP addresses. You can also find the exact number of times a container is accessed and which user issued a certain request.

You will gain an insight on which requests are slow and, in the case of network errors, you can investigate if a certain request did reach the server or did not.

In addition to the customizable charts available on the Azure portal, there are many third-party tools that allow you to access and view Analytics data in a user-friendly way, such as Azure Storage Metrics and CloudBerry Log Viewer. The easiest, yet most powerful, way is to open the raw files using Microsoft Excel where you can create your own views and charts.

 Windows Azure Storage Analytics SDP package is a package that allows you to gather and download all of the log data in a user-friendly fashion. For more information, you can check it on `http://blogs.msdn.com/b/kwill/archive/2014/02/06/` `windows-azure-storage-analytics-sdp-package.aspx`.

Common practices

When building Azure cloud applications, it is very important to understand the specific features each service offers. It is also very important to know the scalability and performance targets for the different components in order to avoid throttling your apps.

Understanding **Service Level Agreements (SLAs)** is crucial to estimate how much downtime your application will pass through and be able to handle these transient faults.

For the best performance, collocate your application and storage in the same affinity group, and enable geo-replication for disaster recovery.

> For full Azure subscription and service limits, quotas, and constraints, you can check out the following document:
>
> `https://azure.microsoft.com/en-us/documentation/articles/azure-subscription-service-limits/`
>
> SLA for most Azure percentages can be found here:
>
> `http://azure.microsoft.com/en-us/support/legal/sla/`

Summary

This chapter has familiarized you with Azure Storage Analytics, which are tools to monitor and trace requests made to your storage account. It has also given you solutions to make your application more robust and resilient to failure by applying retry behaviors against transient faults. To dive deeper into the topics mentioned, you can find a lot of resources on MSDN.

Index

Resource Not Found error 26
RowKey 56

S

Server Message Block (SMB) protocol 78
Service Bus Queues 68
service catalog poster
  URL 2
Service Level Agreements (SLAs) 96
Service Management REST APIs
  about 9, 10
  Microsoft Azure Management Libraries 12
  operations 10
  request 10
  response 11
Software as a Service (SaaS) 1
storage accounts
  about 5
  endpoints 5
  features 5
  logging 7
  metrics 7
  namespace 5
  redundancy options 7
  security 6
Storage Analytics
  about 91
  data, analyzing 96
Storage Analytics logging
  about 91, 94, 95
  log format 95
Storage Analytics Metrics
  about 91, 92
  capacity metrics 94
  transaction metrics 93
Storage Blob service
  blobs 22
  containers 22
  storage account 22
storage services
  about 3
  blob storage 4
  file storage 4
  queue storage 4
  table storage 4

Storage Services REST APIs
  about 12, 13
  Blob service REST API 14
  File service REST API 15
  Queue service REST API 14
  services 12
  Table service REST API 14

T

table
  creating 41
  entities, adding 42, 43
  querying 48-51
table partition 57
Table service REST API
  about 14
  URL 14
Table storage basics
  about 38
  entities 39
  naming rules 39
three layer architecture, Azure Table storage
  Distributed File System (DFS) layer 57
  Frontend (FE) layer 56
  Partition layer 56
transient fault handling 89
transient faults 89

W

WebDav 82
Windows Azure SDK for PHP 17
write-efficient tables
  designing 60

X

x-ms-request-id header 11
x-ms-version request header 11

Z

Zone-redundant storage (ZRS) 7

Thank you for buying
Microsoft Azure Storage Essentials

About Packt Publishing

Packt, pronounced 'packed', published its first book, *Mastering phpMyAdmin for Effective MySQL Management*, in April 2004, and subsequently continued to specialize in publishing highly focused books on specific technologies and solutions.

Our books and publications share the experiences of your fellow IT professionals in adapting and customizing today's systems, applications, and frameworks. Our solution-based books give you the knowledge and power to customize the software and technologies you're using to get the job done. Packt books are more specific and less general than the IT books you have seen in the past. Our unique business model allows us to bring you more focused information, giving you more of what you need to know, and less of what you don't.

Packt is a modern yet unique publishing company that focuses on producing quality, cutting-edge books for communities of developers, administrators, and newbies alike. For more information, please visit our website at www.packtpub.com.

About Packt Enterprise

In 2010, Packt launched two new brands, Packt Enterprise and Packt Open Source, in order to continue its focus on specialization. This book is part of the Packt Enterprise brand, home to books published on enterprise software – software created by major vendors, including (but not limited to) IBM, Microsoft, and Oracle, often for use in other corporations. Its titles will offer information relevant to a range of users of this software, including administrators, developers, architects, and end users.

Writing for Packt

We welcome all inquiries from people who are interested in authoring. Book proposals should be sent to author@packtpub.com. If your book idea is still at an early stage and you would like to discuss it first before writing a formal book proposal, then please contact us; one of our commissioning editors will get in touch with you.

We're not just looking for published authors; if you have strong technical skills but no writing experience, our experienced editors can help you develop a writing career, or simply get some additional reward for your expertise.

Microsoft Windows Azure Development Cookbook

ISBN: 978-1-84968-222-0   Paperback: 392 pages

Over 80 advanced recipes for developing scalable services with the Windows Azure platform

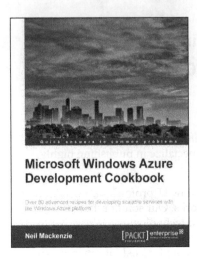

Microsoft Windows Azure Development Cookbook

Over 80 advanced recipes for developing scalable services with the Windows Azure platform

Neil Mackenzie

1. Packed with practical, hands-on cookbook recipes for building advanced, scalable cloud-based services on the Windows Azure platform explained in detail to maximize your learning.

2. Extensive code samples showing how to use advanced features of Windows Azure blobs, tables and queues.

3. Understand remote management of Azure services using the Windows Azure Service Management REST API.

Learning Microsoft Azure

ISBN: 978-1-78217-337-3   Paperback: 430 pages

A comprehensive guide to cloud application development using Microsoft Azure

Learning Microsoft Azure

A comprehensive guide to cloud application development using Microsoft Azure

Geoff Webber-Cross

1. Build, deploy, and host scalable applications in the cloud using Windows Azure.

2. Enhance your mobile applications to receive notifications via the notifications Hub.

3. Features a full enterprise Azure case study with detailed examples and explanations.

Please check **www.PacktPub.com** for information on our titles

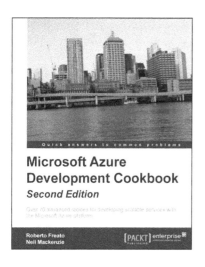

Microsoft Azure
Development Cookbook
Second Edition

ISBN: 978-1-78217-032-7   Paperback: 422 pages

Over 70 advanced recipes for developing scalable
services with the Microsoft Azure platform

1. Understand, create, and use the hosting
   services of Azure for processing and storage.

2. Explore different approaches to implement
   scalable systems by using Azure services.

3. Pick the appropriate automation strategy and
   minimize management efforts.

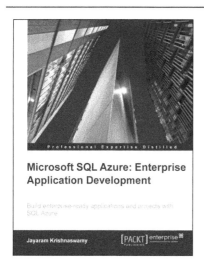

Microsoft SQL Azure: Enterprise
Application Development

ISBN: 978-1-84968-080-6   Paperback: 420 pages

Build enterprise-ready applications and projects with
SQL Azure

1. Develop large scale enterprise applications
   using Microsoft SQL Azure.

2. Understand how to use the various third
   party programs such as DB Artisan, RedGate,
   ToadSoft etc developed for SQL Azure.

3. Master the exhaustive Data migration and Data
   Synchronization aspects of SQL Azure.

Please check **www.PacktPub.com** for information on our titles

www.ingramcontent.com/pod-product-compliance
Lightning Source LLC
Chambersburg PA
CBHW060154060326

40690CB00018B/4112